"I was surprised by this brave, beautiful book, which I will from now on keep by my side for comfort and inspiration. As a long-time Buddhist, terms like 'God' and 'soul' are not so usual, but Karen's use of them in harmony with sayings of great mystics, West and East, gives them new life. And it is especially her eloquent affirmations of the divine as the life force and love force within oneself and every being that resonate with the buddha essence and the diamond clearlight of freedom that sustains our infinite lives. Enjoy this daring book of affirmations—once you get over worrying about feeling way better about yourself, you will find yourself happy at home in it!"

Padma Shri Dr. Robert Thurman
author and translator; Professor Emeritus of Indo-Tibetan Buddhology, Columbia University; Co-Founder of Tibet House US, the Dalai Lama's Cultural Center in America

"This healing, strengthening, empowering collection of wisdom is exactly what my spirit has hungered for. *Sacred Landscapes of the Soul* sits with my journal, ready for my morning inspiration and my evening reflection."

Laurie Halse Anderson
New York Times bestselling author of *Shout*; *Chains* and *Speak*, National Book Awards finalists

"Calling in maelstroms of emotions and heartache, shadows and light, spiritual practitioner Karen Brailsford offers a rich banquet of meditations and images to awaken, calm, challenge and excite soul, mind, heart and body. Plentiful food for all the hungry— indeed starving—souls in our chaotic world today!"

Rev. Matthew Fox
author of *Original Blessing, Christian Mystics* and *The Tao of Thomas Aquinas: Fierce Wisdom for Hard Times*

"*Sacred Landscapes of the Soul* is like a spirited choir singing the wisdom of the ages. It is grounded in intelligent thoughts from the great spiritual writers and song-makers and offers inspiring and transformative guidance. Read it to have your mind and heart opened up. Use it as a contemporary, unaffiliated prayer book or meditation guide."

Thomas Moore
author of *Care of the Soul* and *Ageless Soul*

"It is rare when you read something that reminds you of who you are and brings you back to your essence when you forget. This is such a book. Karen invokes our spiritual ancestors and springboards off them to guide us, step-by-step, through the journey in the wilderness. Expect to encounter refreshing bursts of hope, life and joy, as well as affirmation of the good in the world and our place in it. When I read it, my soul sighed, 'Thank you!'"

Crystal Chan
compassion activist, author of *Bird* and *All That I Can Fix*

"In *Sacred Landscapes of the Soul*, Karen Brailsford provides a path that inspires the reader to find their 'truth' for themselves. Whoever and wherever you are on the journey, this book brings forth Divine information to grow, expand and align with vibrational energy that's of benefit to all of humanity."

Spring Washam
author of *A Fierce Heart*, founder of Lotus Vine Journeys

"*Sacred Landscapes of the Soul* is a luscious deep dive into self-care, self-love and soul expansion. Gentle yet unwavering, this little treasure is a perfect guide to help you set and re-set your course for full healing and brilliant illumination."

Rev. Julie Moret
minister, Agape International Spiritual Center
author of *What's Your What?: How to Ignite Your Unique Brand*

"*Sacred Landscapes* asserts itself among the proverbial books for the ages. Filled with spiritual insight and wisdom, it beautifully evokes the peace and comfort readily available to us just by our mere acknowledgment. Master Agape Licensed Spiritual Practitioner Karen Brailsford's inspired messages and affirmations light the path on our journey towards, and through, eternal peace."

Michael Bernard Beckwith
founder & spiritual director, Agape International Spiritual Center, author of *Life Visioning* and *Spiritual Liberation*

"For those times when we forget to remember who, where and why we really are, Karen Brailsford gently shepherds us through soulscapes of wonder and reminds us of the 'essence of the Presence,' the 'peace in the promise' and our 'resonance with the rhythm of God.' With her powerful but playful, prophetic yet poetic prose she skillfully and carefully uncovers the layers of the heart and exposes the strength of its vulnerability. She creates and opens up a space for us to frolic and to lie down in green pastures; to find respite in faithful forests and delight in majestic mountaintops; to magically find ourselves suddenly soaring with our spirit over tender tundra, across opulent oceans and beside still waters; to come at last to light on peaceful plateaus where we are invited to 'bask in [our] own glow.' Our cup runs over. Be forewarned: This is inspired writing! Lyrical, mystical, and beautiful and apt to transform our lives while traversing any pages unawares."

Rev. Greta Sesheta
7-Pointed Star Ministries, author of *Poems to Wake Up To*

"Karen Brailsford is an alchemist of personal insight and this book is a spiritual breviary of sorts, filled with hard-earned wisdom and written in a key of deep, abiding devotion. She and her sentences cast a light."

Eli Gottlieb
author of *The Boy Who Went Away*, winner of the Rome Prize

Sacred
Landscapes
of the
Soul

Sacred
Landscapes
of the
Soul

Aligning with the Divine
Wherever You Are

KAREN BRAILSFORD

Wyatt-MacKenzie Publishing
DEADWOOD, OREGON

Sacred Landscapes of the Soul
Aligning with the Divine Wherever You Are

Karen Brailsford

Hardcover ISBN: 978-1-948018-81-4
Softcover ISBN: 978-1-948018-84-5

Library of Congress Control Number: 2020935680

Wyatt-MacKenzie Publishing
DEADWOOD, OREGON

For Leola, my mother,
and Charlie, my father,
who love and support me,
from the other side of the veil.

Contents

LANDSCAPE OF INDECISION
When We Don't Know What To Do

LANDSCAPE OF IMMOBILITY
When We Are Frozen With Fear

LANDSCAPE OF SOLACE
When We Are Seeking Peace

LANDSCAPE OF ANTICIPATION
When We're Contemplating Jumping In

LANDSCAPE OF BIRTH
When We Are Ready to Flower

LANDSCAPE OF ONENESS
When We Remember, Immerse and Emerge

LANDSCAPE OF MISSION
When We Catch A Vision For Our Lives

LANDSCAPE OF SURRENDER
When We Dare to Free-Fall

Every landscape is a state of the soul.

HENRI-FRÉDÉRIC AMIEL

Foreword

Dear Beloved,

What an honor it is for me to introduce you to the spiritual being and writer known as Karen Brailsford whom I have had the pleasure of knowing since eternity. Sacred Landscapes of the Soul *represents her immersion into consciousness. Each word was lovingly poured into her, and as you will soon discover, her cup runneth over.*

Much in the way I have been longing for Karen to accept her position as a conduit for the Divine, I have also been waiting for you. It is my hope that you will deepen and expand—and that others will in turn be inspired by your own creative output and contributions to the world.

You are my beloved, in whom I am well pleased. Thank you and bless you for being me.

With great love and deep delight and affection,
God in You and As You

Introduction

GREETINGS. HELLO. WELCOME. NAMASTE. Ours is a divine appointment. This is only fitting, for what you are about to read is the outgrowth and outpouring of an appointment my own soul diligently kept with the Divine over the course of ten years. Divine design guided me to write the words you are about to discover, and divine design led you here.

Wherever you may fall in your belief systems, wherever you may live in this vast and ever-expanding world, this is a time of great turmoil. When I first had the idea to collect and organize my writings into the work you are now reading, *Sacred Landscapes of the Soul*, the world was erupting—and so was I. Into dance! It was the day after the 2016 American presidential election and many were in a state of apoplectic shock. I posted the following passage on my social media feeds:

> Breathe. Cry. Breathe. Scream. Breathe some more. Then, dance! In the middle of the night I had the urge to blast tunes and move. The energy was powerful.

Release! I'm sure you have your own favorites but Beyoncé's "Love On Top" and Bill Withers' "A Lovely Day" plus lots of Prince worked for me. Now, remember who you are and why you are here. Remember who really has the power and who truly governs you. You are the light. We are the light. Let's shine!

The overwhelming positive responses my post generated revealed that I was tapping into something very real, that my words had the power to both soothe and inspire.

It is also a time of tremendous transformation. Those who possess even an iota of faith are here to light the path for those who are overwhelmed by the chaos of these times. And because I believe that what is happening on the world stage is a reflection of—and a projection of—what is transpiring *within*, it's more critical than ever that we clear up what's happening inside of ourselves. Only when we roll up our spiritual sleeves, draping and ragged as they may be, and set about doing the inner work of healing, can we each become a magnanimous and beneficial presence on the planet.

This is where I believe *Sacred Landscapes* can help—to assuage, to comfort, to restore, to bridge the gap between one's faith and one's fear.

The 111 passages that comprise *Sacred Landscapes* are grouped into nine different landscapes within three distinct terrains. An opening and a closing blessing serve to frame them. I was in high school when I first read what is still to this day one of my favorite reflections, penned by transcendentalist Henry David Thoreau: "I have traveled much in Walden." These simple and profound words suggest that one can travel great emotional and psychological distances without embarking on a physical trip. This notion intrigued me then—and intrigues now, hence *Sacred Landscapes of the Soul* as my title. Each of us is a mainland. Every landscape connotes a specific sense of place, a geography and topography that can be explored and mined for inner awareness. I am inviting you to take a stroll in a metaphysical, metaphorical Walden. Please note: although some of the pieces were initially written to coincide with specific holidays or seasons, they will resonate whenever you read them. After all, one can hit the reset button in one's life at any given point within a year, not only in January—and why not celebrate the season of light *any* day of the year, not just at Christmas and Hanukkah? Christmas in July? How about Christmas in April or May or September?

If one were to read through *Sacred Landscapes* from beginning to end, a distinct course emerges: I take the reader from times of trouble and indecision to a deeper recognition of the Divine within. This is not meant to suggest that you should move through the nine identifiable landscapes in successive order, as if you're accelerating on an entrance ramp, or running a relay race with an end goal in mind. Instead, life may catapult you into these landscapes in any number of sequences, or you may experience a few different landscapes simultaneously. For instance, at some point in life, you may feel an overwhelming sense of fear (Forest), come to a fathomless spiritual realization (Ocean)—and then later encounter other challenges that force you to circle back to the fear. Such is the human condition.

Be gentle with yourself. Spiritual transformation doesn't necessarily announce itself with the brio of a burning bush (although I have experienced such wondrous brazenness when it comes to connecting with Spirit). It can come about with stealth. It's a gradual unfolding, like a leaf's metamorphosis from tree limb nestler to cascading color-bearer, floating through the air as it awaits a cushioned landing upon pillowy grass. It's bound to happen, even if you aren't always fully cognizant of each stage during the process.

I believe that words on a page carry a vibration. Feel your way through the landscapes. Allow your fingers to travel down the page while perusing the table of contents. Or simply thumb through the book and see where you land. You are embarking on an adventure and you will end up exactly where you need to be.

Most of the pieces in *Sacred Landscapes of the Soul* are written in the second or third person. However, several—twenty-five to be exact—appear in the first person and are indicated in color and bold, italicized type. The words flowed through me as if they were being communicated directly by God, speaking directly to me. And thereby, to you. It seemed only natural that God would speak boldly and with a flourish.

When I think of God, I think of a life force, a creative agent, an invisible presence. And because I believe that God is gender-neutral and non-binary, I tend to use the pronoun "It." To those uncomfortable with the word "God," feel free to substitute the Ineffable, Spirit, the Divine, Love, Supreme Being, Higher Power, Divine Intelligence, Love Intelligence, Divine Beauty, the Most High, Almighty Presence, Mother-Father-God...whatever floats your Spirit. I use various names interchangeably throughout the text but God is my go-to. I am also particularly partial to the word "Spirit." This conjures up the image of an invisible yet palpable presence that is so close, it is impossible to distinguish where It ends and one begins.

My own journey began at Fort Motte Baptist Church, a small storefront church in the South Bronx, where draped in a white gown and turban I underwent full-body immersion in a baptismal pool at the age of thirteen. My family's attendance at Fort Motte arose out of a covenant. As she lay dying, my maternal grandmother made my mother promise that she would enroll my younger sister and brother and me in Sunday school.

Up until that time, we attended church once a year, on Easter Sunday. I remember sitting in the pew rapturous over my glistening pigtails, shiny patent leather shoes, and new dress complementing the pastel eggs we had dyed the previous night.

At first Mommy would walk us to the door and then scamper away. When several weeks later the Sunday school teacher suggested she stay for service, she did exactly that. And never left. Fort Motte became her home. On rare occasions my father would stagger in, hopped up on spirits, and perhaps Spirit, too, and play the piano. He was a gifted, intuitive player. I cannot listen to Bill Withers' "Lean on Me" without thinking of him. I have no doubt that today, even in death, my mother shows up on Sunday mornings to march down the aisle with the choir and that my father takes his place at the piano from time to time.

At Fort Motte, which was led by a pastor with the uncanny, eucharistic name of Reverend James Goodwine (though on Communion Sunday we sipped grape juice), I witnessed all manner of mysticism and ecstasy. My mother, a regal woman with an easy laugh, would begin to sway uncontrollably to the strains of organ music. Then suddenly, Mommy was prostrate on the burgundy-carpeted floor. Ushers dressed in white nurse's uniforms leapt up to form a protective circle around her and waved cardboard fans with Popsicle handles advertising funeral homes in her direction. Shouting "hallelujah" in between deceptively gibberish incantations, she prophesied and made assurances of good health to ill congregants. Once I asked her after such a spectacle what it felt like to be "slain in the Spirit." She paused momentarily and then quietly replied, "Like flying, like flying."

Each year I placed at the top of my list of resolutions the vow to be closer to God.

In college, I attended Black Church at Yale, which was housed at the Afro-American Cultural Center. On Saturday nights, my fellow undergrads and I gyrated and gesticulated to Madonna, Michael Jackson and Prince. Come Sunday morning those very same halls became hallowed as we threw up our hands in exultation to the sweet sounds of the Yale Gospel Choir and the wailing of Rev. Dwight D. Andrews' saxophone. As co-chair of the hospitality committee, I was tasked with early morning runs to Dunkin' Donuts to pick up refreshments for the congregants, mostly students. The church service provided much needed solace and inspiration while immersed in the rigors of academic study. I can still hear the magnificent choir's rendition of "We've Come This Far by Faith" reverberating in my heart and soul.

Today I attend the racially diverse trans-denominational Agape International Spiritual Center in Los Angeles. A licensed spiritual practitioner since 2009, I pray with congregants, hold vigil during services, offer private counseling and write for *Inner Visions: A Guide for Daily Inspiration*, the center's monthly magazine.

I was guided to Agape in 1995 upon the recommendation of an acupuncturist whom I was seeing so as to shrink fibroid tumors naturally. I had no idea that the healing I would come to experience was beyond the physical. Incredibly, stretched out on the table during a session, I experienced something akin to what I had frequently witnessed at Fort Motte.

After the acupuncture needles gently pierced my skin, a ripple of energy burst through me. I began to tremble and sing spontaneously songs from my childhood church.

"Do you work with Spirit?" I asked the acupuncturist.

During my very first service at Agape (since I had studied ancient Greek, I knew the meaning of the word ἀγάπη—the love of God for man and of man for God), I was overwhelmed by the palpable love. I began to cry, to sway. Instead of a still, small voice, I heard a loud, booming command: "Stand up!" I canvassed the cavernous warehouse where services were held. These words came not from the pulpit but from the depths of my soul.

And then, I was flying.

This same authoritative voice awakened me the next Sunday morning when I decided that I'd much rather remain in bed. "Get up! Michael has a message for you!"

"Michael" was Agape's founder, Rev. Michael Bernard Beckwith, whose fast and fiery intonations reminded me of those of a Baptist preacher. However, the spiritual center espouses "ageless wisdom" and "New Thought" beliefs, which I recognized I had unwittingly ingested in high school while reading the works of Thoreau and fellow transcendentalist Ralph Waldo Emerson, who greatly influenced this school of thought. These beliefs are aligned with my own inherent ones: God is indwelling; and because God is indwelling, I do not have to seek It so much as I have to remember It and my connection to It. I have finally made good on my perennial New Year's resolution.

I consider myself to be "spiritual" rather than "religious." I have encountered God in a synagogue during Rosh Hashanah services and in the playful smile of the Dalai Lama at a conference in India.

The Presence was clearly visible to me at a techno-cosmic rave mass held at Rev. Matthew Fox's University of Creation Spirituality in Oakland, and in the lyrics of the legendary Rev. Andraé Crouch, whose songs I sang as a member of the Sunbeam Choir at Fort Motte (I interviewed both men for *People* magazine).

I felt Spirit whenever I impulsively dropped into St. Patrick's Cathedral for a meditative moment while in New York. In the months before Paris' Notre Dame was engulfed in flames, I visited on Easter and then again at

Christmas when I was inexplicably compelled to attend services there. I sense the Presence in the personal messages I receive from the Persian poet Hafiz, in the way my hand moves instinctively across a canvas when I paint, in the way my writing comes through (like a dam bursting or a steady stream into which I effortlessly glide) and in the synchronicity that follows me everywhere. I have detected God in the whispered murmurings of trees I have had the good fortune to commune with in the stillness of forests. I can personally attest that the mystic scientist George Washington Carver was correct when he postulated that nature spills her secrets if you talk to her.

I honestly do not think what you call It matters, or even if you believe in It. It exists—a divine energy that expresses Itself uniquely in and as everyone and everything. This much I know: That energy birthed the book you are holding in your hands, long before I had the idea that my individual ruminations on the page would someday come together into something greater. When you allow It to guide you, It will take over.

The various selections are meant to serve as meditations, prayers, contemplations, devotionals, psalms, balms. Each has an epigraph that informs the passage and concludes with an affirmation I call "PeakSpeak." Say each one aloud to help anchor the message you are sending to your soul. Speak your spiritual evolution or growth into existence!

PEAK
SPEAK

So why am I here, now, with you?

It is my intention to meet you, the reader, where you are emotionally and spiritually.

It is my intention for *Sacred Landscapes of the Soul* to serve as a comforting voice and a gentle reminder of your innate prowess in handling—and surrendering to—what is.

It is my hope that you will want to return to the various selections repeatedly, and that each reading will touch you in different and unexpected ways, and deepen you in ways you did not think possible upon entering into each dance with them.

It is my intention that *Sacred Landscapes of the Soul* will help carry you through the grit of life so that you are floating on grace and engendering growth along the way—all with a sense of gratitude. For everything. And by "everything," I do mean *every*thing; for everything—the good, the bad, the ugly, the sublime—is working together in a dynamic way for your highest good, refining you but certainly not defining you.

It is my intention that *Sacred Landscapes of the Soul*, encompassing rushing rivers and mountainous peaks, barren wilds and wide-open vistas, verdant spaces and desert paths within the heart, will lead you into radiance, splendor, light. May your soul flow and grow deep like the river. May we flow into one another.

Poem

You Will Find Your Destiny

You will find your destiny in longitudes and latitudes
in pronouncements of truth, in seemingly simplistic
*   platitudes*
in the vicissitudes of life, in ferocious rains and in
*   hurricanes*
in broken cups fused together with gold
You drink, and it is you who runneth over.

In silence you will find solace, in slumber you will
*   seek and arrive*
at an awakening of your soul cajoling you to move
*   forward*
to forge a path, to build sandcastles
to excavate and propagate
to remember and disassemble
all of the broken bits, and to reconfigure them
into a renewed wholeness

You will believe again, you will dance again
You will love again, you will accept love once again
You will find your destiny in unfamiliar terrain
in the slopes and in the downpours
in the downbeat and in the refrain

Life will come full throttle, shaking you to the core
        of your foundation
You will become so rooted you will be grounded
while levitating and catapulting through
        emotional depths
criss-crossing beaten paths until
        the final approach

A multitude of doors and choices are available unto
        you now and forever more
You get to choose how to be with discovery and
        anticipation,
With disappointment and loss, with despair and joy
You will find your destiny within your aspirations
and reservations slowly, deliberately, intentionally
You will find your destiny because you will find you
You will come home.

Opening Blessing

Invitation

AND NOW WE BEGIN AGAIN. We remember everything that has taken place so that we can transmute and transcend. We place everything that has gone before—the regrets and hurts, the elations and the joys—into an amniotic sac and we allow possibility to emerge. We are excited about what we are yet to birth into the world. We are rapturous over the thing that has yet to unfold. There is so much yearning to be made manifest! There is so much love awaiting your fierce nurturing.

A new cycle is beginning and all things are possible because you are surrendering, fluid in the realization of your own realization. You are meant to resonate with the future. Ah, balance. Ah, peace. You become a devotee of your own consciousness.

But first you must make amends with your past. Take your indiscretions and fling them like a shooting star so that they are carried away into universal intonations of both muted and blaring thanksgiving. You must release them for they no longer serve you. And yet they have blessed you with awakenings; you can be grateful.

To see a World in a Grain of Sand
And a Heaven in a Wild Flower
Hold Infinity in the palm of your hand
And Eternity in an hour

WILLIAM BLAKE

Allow your gloriousness to worship you as you become an incandescent lamp unto your feet, hands and heart. Pour tenderness into every thought. Let the wax of your waning denials drip, drip, drip until you want for nothing and ask for nothing. Be emptied of your self-doubt and fear. Dear God, stand in harmony with your majesty! You no longer have to walk the tightrope between your ignorance and your sovereignty, your bliss and the blight of the world. Nothing is taut when you choose to meld your wild unbelief with your subjugated awareness. It is all-flowing and fluid-sensory overload as you drown in your reminiscences and move forward from there into blinding potential. Life begins now.

PEAK
SPEAK

I begin again and again and again, refreshed, revitalized and renewed. I have everything I need because I am life made manifest. And it all begins with me and my belief.

LANDSCAPE OF ENTRAPMENT

When We Are in the Thick of It

LANDSCAPE OF INDECISION

When We Don't Know What To Do

LANDSCAPE OF IMMOBILITY

When We Are Frozen With Fear

The Calm Within the Chaos

WE ARE NOW IN THE EYE OF THE STORM. We are at the crossroads. We are at the intersection where humanity meets divinity, and now we are ready to birth a new creature—our own inimitable, surrendered, empowered selves. This storm has been brewing throughout the ages. It has ravaged flesh and societies, and waged catastrophic wars. It has devalued, disrupted, corrupted and caused destruction. It has been called evil and the devil. It has captured the hearts, the minds and the attention of the many. But no more.

We have been called to awaken from our soul slumbering, and to see and be what's really real. We are ready to pierce the veils of illusory perception and to focus on what it is we want to call forth: love, peace, prosperity, joy, unity, oneness, compassion, fulfillment.

Together we are walking through the storm—arm in arm, soul to soul—and into kaleidoscope rainbows.

We can see clearly now. Just beyond the horizon, in what has been called the Promised Land, lies our destiny. It is less a geographical place and more of a metaphysical heart space. There, we bathe the feet of our so-called enemies, those who do not think as we do, look as we do, walk in the world as we do. There, we allow these so-called others to anoint our heads with oil, recognizing that we are each the Christ-ed self. No one denomination or philosophy or sex holds greater dominion. No one outside of ourselves can dictate our individual purpose or our beliefs—not our parents, or our government or our spiritual teachers. We find truth for ourselves. Then and only then can we luxuriate in our oneness. We both welcome and celebrate our differences. We embody grace. We are healed.

PEAK
SPEAK

I am the embodiment of peace.
I bring the calm wherever I go.

Forest

Maelstrom of Emotions

LOVE. ANGER. TEARS. FORGIVENESS. FEAR. LIGHT. TRUTH. These frequently flow all at once through our consciousness, then pour from our lips without any filters or any sense of decorum. Unfettered, they spill onto our plates— and those of our friends and families and lovers, too. They simply will not mind their manners. Yuck!

It's called being human. Just as a toddler tugs at his mother's skirt to have his needs met, our emotions— catalyzed by a palpable sense of urgency—cry out for attention. "Hold me, honor me," they plead. The good-grace news is that at our core, we are buoyed by the faith of the hemorrhaging woman who touched the hem of Jesus' garment. We know we are meant to heal and be healed—now!

How perfect, then, that in this smorgasbord called life, emotions are always on the menu, tempting us with their juicy flavors. Want to ingest some truth with a little love on the side? Then order it. This low-calorie dish is guaranteed to keep you toned. Feel like dining on some forgiveness? You're well on your way to gourmand status! Or perhaps that entrée of rage looks tempting. Try it, you'll like it—for now, that is. Later, as you pack on the pounds and your arteries clog with untruths, you may have regrets.

But please, don't beat up on yourself. It's all working together for good. And besides, you can always wash it down with a cocktail of tears and self-love, or whittle it away with some prayer and meditation. You see, there's no way you can ever pick a bad dish off the emotional menu. Each meal promises nourishment for the soul as you feast on the irrefutable truth—you are love and you are loved. In the end, you'll always walk away feeling satisfied.

Tantrums and Threats

DON'T YOU KNOW THAT IF YOU GIVE GOD a deadline to deliver on your desires, God will respond? Immediately and without hesitation, as if you had calmly suggested that the two of you meet in a designated spot at a mutually determined time for the taking of a toast and tea?

It can't help but do so. This is Its nature.

Don't you know that if you rant at God over what you don't have until you're so hoarse it feels as if your esophagus is lined with sandpaper, you will hear a booming voice? This voice, a raspy vibrato, bridges the dissonance between your belief and your unbelief. It ferries you across the purgatory where everything in your bones is telling you that if you are here, then God must be over there somewhere—because you sure can't see It, hear It or feel It. Not now. Not ever.

It can't help but do so. This is Its nature.

Don't you know that if you are ever so brazen as to demand, "Why hast thou forsaken me?" you will alight from the cross of your victimization and become airborne?

It can't help but free you. This is Its nature.

You see, whenever you are in a state of tantrum-throwing, threat-making derision, a state of grace inevitably follows. And here's the unheralded truth: It also precedes it. For just as God is everywhere, grace is everywhere.

God's loving arms cradle you from birth to death to rebirth. Its dewy countenance melts in your presence. And there is no way you could ever rage against the machine, life, or God, for that matter, and not have God smile upon seeing you—Its very reason for existence—and run straight into your arms.

PEAK
SPEAK

I am one with God's love and God's grace. I embrace it all now, secure that I am undeniably, irrevocably loved by the Most High always and ever.

Good Morning, Heartache

TO PRAISE THE LIGHT AND THE RADIANCE, to sing praises for all that is good and blessed, to be carried by the holiest of streams and then stand shimmering under waterfalls cascading pure love—this is why we kneel at the altar of thanksgiving.

But in order to lie prostrate in gratitude, so much so until the only prayer you ever say is thank you, well, this is why we must also be grateful for dappled things. Those things that aren't pristine and overtly praise-worthy. Those things that come speckled and spotted, and appear to be covered with blemishes. Those things that seem to deny and contradict the inevitable, undeniable truth: the crooked path will be made straight and healing is happening regardless of diagnoses and yes, even death. Those things that seem to fly in the face of the Ineffable, for the truth is: God is in the midst of everything and every situation.

You see, you've got to praise it, love it, bless it, sanctify it and speak it. You've got to bask in it, dance with it, sing it and strum it—regardless of how it looks, regardless of how it feels. Whether it's up or down, good or bad, pretty or pretty darn ugly—it's thank you, thank you, thank you all the time!

Thank you, Holy Spirit, for this heartache, for now I can learn to pick the strings of my heart and fine-tune them until I am resonant with the music of the spheres.

Thank you, O Holy One, for now I walk by faith, not by sight.

Thank you, Heavenly Father, Mother, God, for the miracle that has already happened.

Thank you, Creator, for the ability to see clearly now that, within the blight, I can find bliss.

PEAK
SPEAK

I give thanks for all that I am, for all that is happening, and for my Greater-Yet-To-Be!

Rage and Release

THESE ARE THE QUESTIONS TO ASK IN TIMES of despondency and rage: How can I be present with what is and still hold fast to faith and joy? How can I transcend belief and enter a state of knowing and grace? How can I love more?

Release the thought that there is something in need of healing, revealing or fixing. Yield not to doubt and overwrought circumspection or introspection. While it can be seductive to meander the depths of your being, exploring past regrets and future possibilities, now you can become rooted in what is now. All is well now so you can celebrate now, give thanks now.

From this now place, you dare to venture into your very own destiny by coming to terms with your connection to the power that is always radiating and acting as a beacon to everyone around you. Your heart already knows it, your synapses already know it, your soul already knows it. All that remains is for your mind to know it.

You can either wrap your mind around your heart, or jettison the mind altogether. You can contort your thoughts into acrobatic feats of mortal morality and rigidity, or you can become fluid like the oceans and let love wash over you again and again. It's the only thing that truly matters, this love. And it will not conform to the mind's idea of right and wrong, of strength and weakness, of respect and irreverence. Love knows no bounds, so allow it and be free. The answers are within. Let them rise up from the depths of your awareness and be in thanksgiving. It's so easy to fall in love with everything and everyone when you are feverishly loving your own divine self. And so it is. And soul it is!

PEAK SPEAK

I am free because I choose to be free! I am always receiving and giving love and expressing gratitude! I am love itself!

Shadow and Light

THE SEMBLANCE OF REALITY IS COMPELLING. We have before us figments inhabited by stark, convincing evidence that life is messy and meandering, frightening and fleeting. It's so easy to be swept away by tides of anxiety and fervid desolation. The deafening chants of polarization may sound louder than the voices of harmony, peace and joy. It's easy to be fooled, it's even easier to be seduced. The siren songs of disruption and chaos beckon.

It's time to tune them out and consider: What is it that you are broadcasting into the echo chamber of the world's heart in this moment? Are you helping to heal the earth's biosphere by infusing it with powerful, transcendent truths? Such as: Change is happening. Something new is making a brave birth into existence. We are redirecting the tide by coursing with it, and then allowing our intention for goodness, grace, fairness and equilibrium to overtake everything and anything.

Or are you adding, whether deliberately or unwittingly, to the maelstrom by failing to remember that this, too, shall pass?

And the earth was without form, and void;
and darkness was upon the face of the deep.
And the Spirit of God moved upon the face
of the waters. And God said, Let there be light:
and there was light.

GENESIS 1:2-3

Wake up! We have been here before. There is nothing new happening here. Raging fear has previously clouded our vision and cast its shadow time and time again. It is the nature of human history to ebb and flow. It is our nature, too. We will be catapulted past this time of tremendous shift and its accompanying birthing pains into one of unprecedented creation and awakening. The milk of human kindness will flow unimpeded.

Now is not the time for subterfuge or willful ignorance. We cannot unsee what we have seen, no matter how insurmountable or scary it may appear. We cannot bargain with half-truths and flagrant misperceptions. We have come for such a time as this! We are ready. We will triumph. We need only remember: We are love. We are loved.

PEAK
SPEAK

I pierce through the veil of illusions and see light everywhere! I bring the light!

More Than Enough

Dear Beloved,

Why do you ignore me? Why do you choose to hide from me, the one who birthed you into existence and sent shooting stars streaming love-light from one galaxy to the next in your honor? Do not deny me. Do not resist me. For when you fail to sing your song, allowing the notes created especially for you by the heavenly spheres to fade into silence, this is exactly what you are doing.

By not bringing forth your gifts (and there are many for I only create dynamic renaissance men and women!), you are in effect stating, "I am not enough." But I am here to tell you that you are more than enough. You are abundance itself.

How many times must I prove myself and demonstrate how much I love you, how much I adore you, how much I look forward to all that we are going to do together? Know that I am here to support you. Let go, let God. Trust. Explore. Create.

As above, so below, as within, so without,
as the universe, so the soul

HERMES TRISMEGISTUS

Own your mysticism. Know that you are your own greatest teacher. Look within. Find me there. Surrender. Shine your light. Soar. Be the spark for others. For together, we can light up the sky and birth a brand new planet, a new star, a whole new dimension.

The key, dear hearts, is to own your power, for in doing so you change your life and the lives of every man, woman and child. Nature itself feels your impact. Every blade of grass is made more luminous. Clouds reconfigure and take on new shapes. The grains of sand sparkle more brilliantly. See how powerful you are?

What grand purpose is calling you? Let love be your guide and enjoy the symphony!

Love,

God In You and As You

PEAK
SPEAK

When I bring forth my gifts,
I honor that which created me.

Spiraling

THERE IS A TENDENCY TO BELIEVE that life is linear. We travel through the phases of existence pausing here, stopping there, skipping, sauntering, running, and yes, at times, colliding, tripping and falling, from one stage to the next. We think that as we matriculate from one experience to the next, we accumulate knowledge that will catapult us into a rarefied place, an exalted state. From this perspective, life is an obstacle course, or a maze. We earn grades and we graduate once we've run the race or stumbled out of the tangled web we weave. Grace equals gratitude plus Now I Know Better Because I've Been There Before and I Certainly Won't Do *That* Again. Thank God.

But what if up is down and down is up? In other words, consider that instead of soaring we're meant to simply spiral (though mounting up with wings like eagles is a lovely visual and a high-flying aspiration). We spiral deep. Deep into the gap that exists between who we really are and who we think we are, or even ought to be. Deep into the swirls of the infinity circle. Deep into God.

What if what appears to be that same old problem rearing its ugly head again, that same old issue we thought we'd put to bed, is actually an opportunity for God to command us to "take up thy bed, and walk?" Again and again. Every resurrected issue then becomes the pathway to remembered wholeness and oneness, a way for us to be resurrected.

You see, there is no direct route to get to where we are going because we're already there. We are already home free. And as Dorothy so brilliantly recognized, there's no place like home. We've got it all, we know it all, we are already It.

PEAK
SPEAK

As I soar on the wings of Spirit I deepen into the awareness that every experience helps me grow in God.

Longing

MORE BASIC THAN OUR NEED FOR FOOD, shelter and water is the hunger for that which can only ever truly satisfy our souls—the longing to know the Divine. This longing gives us life and purpose and passion. Whether we are conscious of it or not, it's always propelling us forward.

It was longing that catalyzed and alchemized into the great books of spirituality. We came, we saw, we communed. Longing invites us to pose the very same question that Elizabeth Barrett Browning asks in her romantic sonnet: How do I love thee? Simply substitute "God" or "me" for "thee." Longing urged each of us to stand in our own faith and brilliance and declare, "Let me count the ways."

And the ways, they, too, are innumerable! They can be seen in every work of art from the pyramids to the Picassos. They can be distilled in every verse of every song. For we get to see God by creating, whether it's one of the Seven Wonders of the World, a magnificent painting—or our own lives.

Blessed are the pure in heart:
for they shall see God.

MATTHEW 5:8

But here's the curious thing: Sometimes the longing shows up masked as the desire for a bigger house, a better job, a faster car or a soulmate who meets all of our needs. We think we want more, more, more, when, in actuality, we want to have a relationship with God and by definition, with ourselves.

Through spiritual practice and soulful play, we purify ourselves by stripping away the illusion that more is more. We discover what's real. And since God is the only thing happening—in fact, It is *the* happening—the desire to see God up close and personal rests at the heart of every dream, every coin tossed into the fountain. So make your wishes now and be blessed.

PEAK
SPEAK

When I live a creative, on-purpose life
I meet God face-to-face.

When Things Fall Apart

Dear Beloved,

The center cannot hold but I can and will continue to hold you. I draw you close and into me. I relish the very thought of you. I explore the depths of your soul. Ours is a sojourn of innocents. There are no guilty ones, only the forgotten ones who scream and hurt, and languish and perish from little or no contact with their divinity.

But I am here to tell you, do not be moved by these protestations of inhumanity. You were never and will never be human—despite blood, bone, muscle and tissue. You are so much more than flesh. You are so much more than emotion and thought. You are capable of wondrous things and despite appearances to the contrary, wondrous things are happening, even now. Even now as you brandish weapons and wail. Even now as your senses falter and things seem to be falling apart. Even now as lives grow dank and go dark.

I will not be denied. Love will not be denied. Surrender unto the grace and the peace encoded in your DNA.

Love is the Divine Mother's arms;
when those arms are spread,
every Soul falls into them.

HAZRAT INAYAT KHAN

These strands of love have the capacity to coil and snake from heart to heart, person to person, soul to soul, creating a living, conscious chain of humanity and divinity. At their intersection is a powerful and yet simple message, the very same one I have communicated to you through so many sons and daughters throughout the centuries: Love and be loved. Heal and be healed. Allow grace to penetrate the shell of your pain and suffering. What will break through—the realization that you are not alone, that despair will be met with comfort when you turn within and when you turn to one another—will bring you to your knees in thanksgiving. I. Am. Here. From here to eternity.

Love,
God In You and As You

PEAK SPEAK

I am the way, the truth and the light—the means by which God shows up on the planet!

Miracle of Miracles

THE ALCHEMY OF LIFE is such that we are eternally burnishing gold and turning clay into muscle and tissue. We fire up our desires and then scatter them into the torrents, or we hurl them into the heavens with egregious abandon—hoping, imploring, begging, beseeching—so that they will latch onto something, anything, of weight, of permanence.

But as it's been said time and time again, the center cannot hold. True believers do not hope or beg or beseech; they conjure. Their prayers become holy temples consecrated with amulets of discovery, knowledge and above all, self-acceptance. Their fingers massage rosary beads of awareness and when they kneel before altars, they are actually bringing heaven down to earth's fluctuating floors. Lassoing the moon is not a whim but a necessary endeavor to propel the planet and accelerate healing.

What to make of these Now times?

These times when one is likely to detect attrition rather than alchemy and actualization? When so many souls are trembling with fear in anticipation of the next terrible thing?

There may be wars and rumors of wars (both inside you and in the world at large), but our task right now is to build a fort of fortitude and forward-thinking perseverance. Be brave in your belief that the consecration of all beings can't help but propel us into a state of shared bliss. Honor everyone's sovereignty, even when they wear crowns of ridicule. Rejoice in the threads of sanguine thought weaving their way through a few chosen ones who refuse to uphold conventional wisdom negativity. Instead, uplift weary doubts with the self-mastery of a venerable being. You are a transformer, a transcendent conduit standing on the precipice of possibility and practicality. See what is not only possible but also palpable when you wield your love with a mighty grace.

PEAK SPEAK

I wield a mighty love that transmutes and transforms. I create miracles wherever I go— and I am everywhere!

Genius and Passion, Fury and Doubt

Dear Beloved,

Cry those tears. They are healing you and fertilizing your biggest dreams, which are manifesting right now. You are in the gathering phase. You are drawing unto you the people, the situations, the inspiration and the insights necessary for realizing your purpose. Your purpose— to come into full alignment with why you are here and how best to deliver your gifts to the world—is the greatest achievement of all.

Can you not see how prepared you have been for this adventure? Can you not see there have been no missteps or mistakes? Everything is for you, even those things that felt painful and treacherous. Especially those things that felt painful and treacherous. They helped to refine you and in no way define you. Who you are was determined at first light—that moment you decided, and yes, it was a decision, to come into existence as flesh and blood with all of the accoutrements that entails: genius and passion, fury and doubt.

Peace, be still.

MARK 4:39

You get to experience it all. And then you get to choose: How will you be with all that is transpiring inside of you, and out in the world? Lately, it appears that the world is spiraling into chaos. Rest assured—everything is in divine order. Will you be in resistance, or will you place your hands together in a prayerful pose, meeting and greeting yourself right where you are? Here, you can simply allow everything to simply be, as you honor all of you. And what a delight you are! It's so easy to deny your wonder when you are wandering in the wilderness! But when you choose to rest within the shade of my love, to seek comfort in me, you will be relieved of all worry and will go forward in love.

Love,

God in You and As You

PEAK
SPEAK

I have everything I need to realize my greatest dreams! I am living my life on purpose!

Morning Promise

THERE WILL COME A TIME WHEN you forget to remember. Perhaps you were dreaming you were awake without promise or restoration. Perhaps you had come to believe that with the knife of futility you could cut away old hurts and transgressions.

Know this much: Love is here. In times of injustice and unforgiveness, in wretched sickness and restless nights. When the square peg strains to fit into the round hole. When your soul contracts unto itself and refuses to step out into the light and the air.

In these times take refuge in the faith you forged when everything appeared to be possible. Take refuge in the comforts you used to know and welcome—enlightened truths harnessed so fastidiously within your tired limbs that you could fling hope into the heavens and catch a glimpse of your soaring potential. Then and only then will you remember.

You will remember the grace of an endless sky.

You will remember dew-damp soil and febrile dreams.

This, too, shall pass.
PERSIAN SUFI POETRY

You will remember the bending of the tree in the wind, as it relaxes into fervent prayer and riotous play.

You will remember to remember that once upon an eternality you floated through density and catapulted into scattering stars.

You will remember life in the invisible: gentle rain that washed away all doubts and timidity, brazen light that fed the hunger of all species and lavish blessings that swept you far, far and away beyond the horizons of your fear.

It was a good life then, when you remembered to remember. You can return to that time of innocent rectitude and conscious fortitude right now. In this moment, at this time, before you open your eyes and venture into the day.

A new adventure awaits you, a new life beckons. You can and will begin again. Today. Now.

PEAK
SPEAK

Every day is a winding road filled with promise and endless possibility! And I am here for it!

Sacred Landscapes of the Soul

IN THE THICKNESS OF THE UNKNOWN it can appear that you are traveling into no man's land. This is true, for no individual has ever gone or will ever go where you traverse.

As you forge ahead on your journey, you will come across diverse terrain. You will meet dense forests and fertile gardens overrun with unfamiliar trees and plants. Stop and smell the roses, for each flower embodies God's grandeur. Notice the way the light shimmer-streams through branches; there are answers in the patterns dancing before you. And should you find yourself at a riverbank, wade in. Some will want to experience full-body immersion. You will either float or find yourself walking on water.

You may even encounter marshlands populated with the skeletal remains of aborted hopes. Say a blessing, for it is possible to resurrect a dream deferred and turn swamps into holy ground. The ancestors will be eternally grateful.

At times, sunken valleys will seem so horrific you forget to breathe. Remember the Twenty Third Psalm—"thou art with me"—then inhale, exhale and pirouette your way onto your next destination. The key is to stay focused by performing the technique known in the dance world as "spotting." Keep your eyes trained on a single thing as you turn your body 360 degrees. This way you won't become dizzy and spin out of control. Here's a hint: If that thing you focus on is God, this works particularly well!

In the end, you will come to a mountaintop, just like Martin Luther King, Jr. Envision locking arms with whomever you claim as your master teacher, take a breath and survey the lands below. It will feel comfortable to rest in this hallowed place. And you may. But dare to leap into the abyss. Soaring high above your troubles and gliding on faith, you will catch a different view. Know that you have arrived.

PEAK SPEAK

I walk hand-in-hand with the Divine and so regardless of the bumps in the road, I believe I can fly!

In Limbo

HAVE YOU EVER FLOATED TENTATIVELY over a seemingly limited selection of choices? Do I turn left or right? Am I to go here or *there*? What is the right decision anyway? In these situations, the call is simply to make one. Propelled by that energy, things in your life will begin to shift.

The fact of the matter is, there are no wrong choices. There is only the best possible decision at any given moment in time, given your experiences, beliefs, faith and spiritual practice (lots of prayer and meditation). This faith can transmute any circumstance, surmount all hurdles and ensure you are staying the course by redirecting the road upon which you journey. In other words, you can't make a bad choice because not only are your steps always guided, the road is, too. The path adjusts to your decisions, swerving and curving to keep you safe and secure.

So take a breath. How does that feel? No doubt the burden of decision-making is made lighter as you begin to take off and soar.

You see, purgatory, that place where you used to dangle in a state of bewilderment and confusion, is not an option. After a while, a plane that hovers will run out of fuel, and so will you. Limbo is limiting. Choose and let the chips fall as they may, for those chips are actually pieces of manna from heaven. They give you energy.

If for some reason, you find yourself regretting your choice, know that you will be presented with another set of circumstances from which you get to choose again, given your experiences, beliefs, faith and spiritual practice. This is the beauty and the thrill of life. It is forever changing, and so are you. You will be resurrected. You can bet on it.

PEAK
SPEAK

The universe supports my every step and is always creating a path for me!

The Love in the Lull

AFTER ALL THE RE-BIRTHING of the holiday season, it's now time to embrace a brand new year. What will it bring, we wonder? What new vision, new person, new thing?

But what if instead of the pa rum pum pum pum of our drum playing—those moments when we deliver our gifts so freely, shine our light so magnificently, and recognize so clearly (just like the little drummer boy), that we have something special to offer—we are met with the humdrum rhythms of day-to-day life?

Do not worry! For in the silence, when nothing seems to be happening, there is tremendous opportunity to hear what is being shouted from the farthest corners of the universe: *"I am with you always!"* The pregnant pause allows for the breath; one is now attuned to the beats in between each and every heartbeat.

For in the stillness, there is no more time for getting and spending. One comes to realize that in not taking a

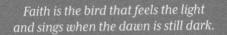

*Faith is the bird that feels the light
and sings when the dawn is still dark.*

RABINDRANATH TAGORE

particular path, a perfect one is forged for us anyhow, somehow. We can't help but get to where our souls want to take us!

You see, that hesitation you might feel is not necessarily born out of paralysis or fear, but out of trust. One trusts that God provides, one trusts that all is well, one trusts that truly all is possible. The seeming quiet allows us to marinate. For there is a love in the lull of nothing appearing to happen in the physical realm. There is resonance in the rhythms of God. The lull is actually a lullaby with which God rocks us into a state of blessed assurance. So instead of making resolutions this new year, let's be resolute in the absolute. Know that in the end, each intention will be fulfilled. For in the end, there is only love.

PEAK
SPEAK

I stand unwavering in the absolute awareness that the universe supports my every heart-felt intention. I trust that all is well. Always!

Love Rushes In

Make room in your hearts for a healing. Prepare a space within your souls for a mighty gathering of divine beings and a holy convergence of situations and circumstances invested in helping to catapult you into the next stage of your life. For now is the time of your great awakening! You will remember!

You will remember those times you were carried and only God's footprints were visible in the sand. You will remember the miracles that materialized out of nowhere, the times when life and love itself seemed to make a way out of no way. And you will take tremendous comfort in all of it, noting, "Life is good. All the time!" And this time you will really mean it.

Perhaps you've been wondering, "What do I do now? Where am I headed?" Well, the answers are all inside. Ponder this instead: "Who am I *really*? What is my divine purpose? Why am I here?" Love will rush in and guide you to the answers. In fact, love *is* the answer.

Faith overtakes fatigue and you can't help but shout for joy. Now you have arrived. You have excavated those rough-edged diamonds within and softened the shards with self-forgiveness and self-love. You have come out blazing because, after all, you are pure light created out of the purest of light. You have peered into the mirror and gazed upon the shining soul staring back at you in wonderment. It's a beautiful life, indeed.

You have let go of everything. Nothing else matters but God. This realization is what will see you through. You have remembered who you are—and you will be bowled over by the very thought, the very glory of you. Love rushes in and fills you to overflowing.

Wow. Wow. Wow!

PEAK
SPEAK

When I allow love to rush in, I am awakened unto the undeniable, indefatigable truth— life is good! All the time. Really.

The Space Between

THERE APPEARS TO BE AN INTRINSIC, biologically driven, human mandate to make things happen. This reflex shows up at birth. We cry because we know that if more capable beings do not feed, clothe and comfort us, we will die. Then, later, as we matriculate through classes and careers, we are taught to study and produce (ideas, things, money!) so we can make something of ourselves. As if we aren't already perfectly made in the image and likeness of God!

Fortunately, sentient sages have always known better. The English Romantic poet William Wordsworth wrote that in "getting and spending, we lay waste our powers." Rumi urges us to "keep walking, though there's no place to get to" and to "move within."

One need only consider Stonehenge or the rose to realize that true creation is not born out of will but from inspiration. And what exactly is inspiration? It means to be breathed by God. Imagine that! Spirit is breathing us right now.

But how can we find that infinite space in between the inhalation and the exhalation—that place where grace takes hold and our deepest wishes manifest—if we're too busy, too consumed or too concerned?

Here's a thought: Let go and let God. Instead of *doing*, make your business about *being*. Trust that your inner child has all of its needs met even before you let out that wail. That's right, it's okay to wail—crying is calisthenics for the soul. Plus, God can handle your tears!

Next, be silent. In surrendering, you can wipe away every doubt and perceived hurt by embalming them with stillness. This is the dawning of the Age of Stillness. There is absolutely nothing for us to do, for our divinity is already a given. **Be still, and know that I am God!**

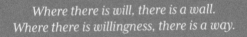

PEAK SPEAK

I won't make a move without my Maker! From morning 'til night, it's all God, all listening, all the time.

Call and Response

THE UNIVERSE IS A DYNAMIC, expansive and responsive field of awareness. Within it, magnificent worlds—realms of consciousness and alignment expressing through the signals that show up in our thoughts—unfold right before our eyes.

How often have you thought of someone, only to have them appear in the flesh minutes later? This is not coincidence. You called it forth! How many times have you dropped down into the seat of your soul, only to have that which you were seeking bubble up after your dance with the Divine? You called it forth!

The universe is not only responsive to your physical and emotional needs. It is so giving and loving, It hears your calls for awareness and understanding of Its very nature. God takes great pleasure in satiating your appetites, fulfilling your needs, and answering your queries—no matter how foolish they might be. It delights in filling your senses so that your cup runneth over. Because you take an interest in *It*, It takes an interest in *you*.

The answers are always as clear as those given to Moses by the burning bush. As Bob Dylan poetically sang, they are blowing in the wind—and you are the wind, the sun and the rain. Or the answers might appear in the passage of a book you are reading right now—and you are the letters and nouns and the verbs in expression. Or perhaps you find your aha moment in a conversation you overhear between two strangers. There are no strangers in God. Each is you. Each is The One. Yes, the answers are all around you. The challenge, then, becomes not to elicit an answer—that's a given— but to know what to ask and how to listen.

PEAK SPEAK

I recalibrate my being so that I am attuned to the word of God. I seek and find answers everywhere I go!

Searching

STOP PEERING INTO EVERY CREVICE and geological forma-
tion for clues to your own unfolding. Clay earth and
solid rock cannot begin to tell the story of how you
are emerging from glory to greater glory. Set aside
your queries and interrogations. You are not a researcher
or an officer of the law when it comes to your soul.
You are a divinely dynamic expression. Yes, it is written
"seek, and ye shall find," but there is no need to seek.
There is no need to make pilgrimages, to run races, to
immerse yourself in texts and treatises, to journey into
the dynamics of your family history or supposed inherited psychoses.

You don't have to do anything. There is no becoming
It or trying to be It. You are already It. There is only the
embracing of who you are and have always been. Cease
the questioning and the berating and remember.
Remember the sensation of the good earth in between
your toes. Remember the warmth of dawn's beatific light

upon your cheek. Remember the breath. Dance to its rhythms. Inhale and exhale mindfully. Universes can be discovered within the pregnant pauses of a breath. Diseases, healed. Answers, revealed. Be here now. Be grateful now. Be emptied now of all your doubts and fill your cup to overflowing with rapturous joy.

This is the only rumination given permission to consume your being: Why am I here? In other words: How can I step out of the shadows and out of my own way and allow? You won't find the answers in far-flung destinations. You won't find it in someone else's story. Seek ye first the kingdom of God. The kingdom is within. Greet it, find solace and marvel at the simple beauty of it all. Welcome home.

PEAK SPEAK

I have already overcome the world and am basking in the glory of me! I meet and greet myself right where I am with love, delight and acceptance.

Choose You This Day

REMEMBER THE TIMES you left your awareness at the door and walked in darkness. Remember the times Spirit wrapped you in Its glory and held fast to the wonder of you. Every day in your life thus far you have awakened to the freshness of a brand new you. Every day you have been granted a most special wish—the wish to live. Now, contained within that wish there is a choice, and within that choice there is a realm of infinite bounty: You have chosen to allow the joy and the hope, and the promise and the passion, to override whatever happened in the yesterday and to begin anew.

In that miraculous moment when you open your eyes, you are being born into pregnant possibility. What will you choose this day? To be, to love, to learn, to remember? How will you walk along the roads of this heaven on earth and call forth what you need this day? Will you plead and cajole, or will you simply pick the fruit from every tree you come across and savor the sweetness? Will you bow in shame or will you stand erect so that the life force can flow through you boundless and free?

What will you choose this day? It's all up to you. It may appear that life is unfolding quite mysteriously, but there is joy in the mystery and there can be peace in the promise of what is just over the horizon. Keep walking, keep marching, keep remembering. You've come this far by faith. Your faith will provide a way out of no way. Be open to the glory that is you. Be grateful for the blessing of being alive in this moment. Then and only then will you truly know how good life is and how great thou art.

PEAK
SPEAK

I choose love and light in each eternal moment!
I bow to the grace in me and live life full out!
Ain't no stopping me now!

The Power of Doubt

As one navigates a spiritual life, one frequently encounters stones and boulders on the path. Sometimes you can simply pick up a pebble and toss it, laughing as you watch it skip over the waters of your experience. At other times, you may feel the muscles in your back ripple as you struggle to push the giant rocks away from the tomb of your heart and give way to your own resurrection.

You may often sense that you are uplifted and inspired by Spirit. But there may be moments when you feel weary. You may find yourself slipping into a chasm of doubt and questioning whether you have lost a grip on your mental faculties. Perhaps that still, small voice you hear in prayer, in meditation, as you drive, as you exercise, as you eat, as you sleep, as you dance, as you knit, as you paint, as you inhale, as you exhale, is irrefutable evidence of dementia. What if you are not a spiritual being having a human experience but a crazed one?

It's in these moments that something greater than incessant mind chatter is finally able to take hold. Instead of clinging to your sanity, spontaneously let go and take a walk in the land of bewilderment. ***"You are my beloved, in whom I am well pleased,"*** you will hear.

Dancing in sync with the music of the spheres, you attune to Spirit. ***"I'm with you always,"*** It says tenderly.

You throw your arms up in jubilation. ***"Ta-da!"*** It exclaims, trumpeting your soul like an illusionist announcing his latest magical feat.

Then, all you can do is praise God for you now know that God is real—real in your soul.

PEAK
SPEAK

No matter what I am thinking or how I am feeling, I can access the truth of my being. God is real and is having Its way with me in each and every moment.

The Answer

AT TIMES IT CAN SEEM DIFFICULT to take things one day at a time, let alone one eternal moment at a time. There is a tendency to want to know what is going to happen and how it is going to happen. The real question to pose, however, is *who* is happening now?

You see, there's no need to confer with your mother, your father, your posse, the constellations, or even a crystal ball. Instead of taking polls and gauging probabilities ad nauseam, you need only look in the mirror to arrive at the truest of answers. But do so only after you have consulted with the miracle of an oracle that indwells you and had a heart-to-heart with the essence of the Presence. For *you* are what's happening; *you* are the answer. It's all inside—the answers to your prayers, your reason for being, hoping and dreaming.

Once you have erected a spiritual tower built on the rungs of meditation, visioning and journaling, once you have prayed the prayer of seeing God, loving God and walking hand-in-hand with God—day by day—you will see in this hallowed mirror a vast and majestic universe. The effects are dazzling! The love-light reflection of God will shine through like a rainbow in your eyes. You will conjure colors never seen before—and embrace your spiritual authority by naming each of them, calling it all good and very good.

There's no need to know what's ahead. Simply get ready to receive. Stand with your arms extended in a posture of gracious receptivity, keeping your eyes tightly closed for as long as possible. It's in the anticipation, in the bated breath, that you will leap into heaven—the eternal now.

PEAK SPEAK

I dwell in the present moment and reside in God, trusting that a glory-filled future is guaranteed. This is my birthright!

Shift

NOW IS NOT THE TIME TO GIVE UP. Now is not the time to bury your desires. It is inevitable that you will receive what you are seeking because you are aligned with your soul's mission. You want what you want because in the time before there was time, the wind whispered to your heart. And your heart spoke back. Together you determined your greatest yet to reveal. You set a date and a time then you went about the business of birth and growth and life. Your desires are not the outgrowth of a random confluence of hopes and dreams. They are your soul's highest calling. You are being called to remember.

Instead of throwing your arms up in frustration, hold up the sky with them in praise. Shape them into a receptacle for all the good, all the love, all the blessings you are finally able to receive. At last. Your doubts evaporate with the realization that you have been here before. You were once lost and empty, only to feel the flow of the

> *Yet if hope has flown away*
> *In a night, or in a day,*
> *In a vision, or in none,*
> *Is it therefore the less gone?*
> *All that we see or seem*
> *Is but a dream within a dream.*
>
> **EDGAR ALLAN POE**

universe sweep you up in a cascade of hope and possibility. This was when you remembered: Grace fell upon me and my faith was restored. A last-minute solution. A glimmer of light in a darkened tunnel. A shaft of radiance in a black night of the soul. A shift. This happened. And because it happened, it can happen and will happen again.

There is an innate part of you that knows everything you need to fulfill your desires. Double down on your faith. Throw yourself into it so passionately you come crashing into ecstasy. You do not have to badger or beseech. It is a given. Your wishes will be granted. Simply know it. Believe it. Trust. Trust life. It is for you.

PEAK SPEAK

I am in divine alignment with my soul's highest calling! I call it forth and it is done! Now!

In Times Like These

Dear Beloved,

Give thanks for the space between. Those periods when the sun appears to take an eternity to rise and the nights are ripe raw. Those times when love seems to elude you by cowering in the shadows and the stars flicker like candles about to be extinguished.

For these are the times that I am at my most mighty. These are the seasons of your soul during which I plant and till, rake and cultivate, and then plant some more. For only then can you flower, rising out of hardened clay. These are the glory days in which I get to work my majesty and recalibrate the heavens, the flow of oxygen, the pulse of the earth, the mitosis of cells, the twisting of DNA strands, the currents of the oceans.

I trust that in the beginning was the word and that you continue to be the co-creator of those words, which together we scribe into sonnets and verses, songs and novellas, novels and treatises. I trust that a stone is a

Out of my dark hours wisdom dawns apace,
Infinite Life unrolls its boundless space.

RAINER MARIA RILKE

stone and a grain of sand is a grain of sand. I trust that
you believe in me even when you do not believe in
yourself. I trust that you are everything and that I am
everything because I am you and you are me. But only
if you know all of this to be so.

All things are possible in the infinite beingness that is
you. Together we are writing the Book of Life. Together
we are eating from the Tree of the Knowledge of Good
and More Good, and birthing orchards and rainforests
into existence. You can see the forest for the trees,
the truth for the falsehoods, the rainbow for the colors.
And together we name it all good and very good.

Love,

God In You and As You

PEAK
SPEAK

As my soul stretches and dances toward God, I trust that grace rules the spaces in between. I have the faith to dip and bend. I am grateful for everything!

You Are the Gift

YOU ARE THE GIFT—resplendent in your resolve to rise above the fury and become anchored in pure dynamic love. This is not the love of the aimless—those who wander in circles over terrains marked by the tread of previous sojourns. This love is actionable, magnanimous and on purpose. It is infused with an ebullient grace. It lifts you up so that you can alight upon others with blessings. It allows you to make an indelible impression that will not be refuted.

The arc of your intention effortlessly catapults you from desire to possibility to revelation. You bring to every situation an impenetrable faith. Even when you do not recall the brazen steps you took without descending into a pit of despair, you are imbued with a trust that knows no bounds. You glide until you became airborne. Within the miasma of your subconscious there is a remembrance of things past, and even of those things to come. You know that you are guided. You see your own light illuminating your path.

Love is life. All, everything that I understand,
I understand only because I love.

LEO TOLSTOY

When you recognize that the riches you seek are contained within, you bask in your own glow. You burn brighter than the sun. Unfamiliar lands do not frighten you. Instead they captivate, for you realize that you are about to embark on an adventure. You are more than ready for this thrill. In fact, you have been waiting for the very moment you get to reveal just how prepared you are. You hold fast to an inner knowing. Everything is going to be all right. You will come through this shining, that much is guaranteed. Within the largesse of your magnificence reigns an undeniable truth: That which you yearn for is already happening. You are a gift to your very own soul. You are grateful.

PEAK
SPEAK

I bring forth the light of my very own soul.
I am a blessing to the world!

Prescription for Constriction and Restriction

Dear Beloved,

There is no cause ever for worry or regret. The decisions you have made are in the past, and the ones you will be called to execute are in the future. Now, in this moment, all is well. In fact, all is divinely perfect. I deem it so and therefore it is so.

Feel the pulsations of the earth through the soles of your feet. You are grounding now. As you stare into the face of your fear you will remember once again how far you've come.

Feel the breath of my love for you in your muscles, your fiber, your whole being. My breath encompasses this galaxy and countless others. It can fire up your will, your hopes and your creativity. It will sustain you now.

Feel the expanse of your love for whatever and whomever it is you love: a favorite song, a treasured memory, another soul who has been able to move you into joy and laughter. Remember and embody. It is possible,

*if you think it so, to transmute the fears that haunt you
now from ghosts into regal angels of possibility.*

*In the realms where you love and live, there is nothing
to fear. In the realms of your holy being there is only pure
dynamic essence. In this state of heightened conscious
awareness, you see beyond substance into every atom;
your vision penetrates the densest and most diabolical of
circumstances. Here, now, your fear dissolves and trust
takes over. Instead of taking the lead, allow yourself to be
carried by my love.*

*I have prepared a special place for you, and deco-
rated it with your own glory. Seek it. Nestle into it. Find
solace there. Discover me within you. Breathe into home.*

Love,

God in You and As You

PEAK SPEAK

**I release all fears and all frustrations!
I stand in trust and rest in God!**

The Power of Love

THE COCOON OF FEAR, worry and denial that has shrouded your heart is cracking at this very moment. The tremors that appear to be causing the earth to crumble beneath your feet are not the result of an earthquake or a heartbreak but a breakthrough. For all ground is holy ground and the fissures are merely figments of an overactive yet under-utilized imagination.

Instead of dreaming big, dream love! It's time to vanquish victimhood. Feel the radiating heat of God's love burst through the layers of your confusion and indecision, and make the only choice that ever need be made—choose love. Uncertain as to how to best nurture your child in a particularly challenging situation? Choose love! Confused as to whether he or she is The One to jumpstart your greatest healing? Choose love! Swayed by appearances of poor health and a diminishing bank account? Choose love! Fearful you won't ever secure that job or that house, or find the road map to a well-lived life? Choose love!

Love will show you the way, taking you over bridges spanning resistance and across fast-churning waters. Do not be afraid to look down for once you do, you will marvel, as did the poet Langston Hughes, at how your "soul has grown deep like the rivers." With each decision, you are expanding. With each hurdle, you are deepening and therefore quickening.

When you finally reach the not-so-distant shores of blessed assurance (it's your destiny!), you will stretch your arms into the heavens and shout "hallelujah." Love in the form of undulating waves of joy and ecstasy will wash over you and your heart will burst. Ah, transformation at last! Choose love! It has created you and It has chosen you.

PEAK
SPEAK

My heart is open wide to love, to life, to God!
I choose my highest good and the highest good
for all by choosing love again and again!

The Road to Blessed Reassurance

TO EVERYTHING THERE IS A SEASON, and a rhyme and a reason. The quiet storms are as valuable as the tempestuous cyclones, and there are hallelujahs in the hurricanes. Yes, praise the sun but in the same breath, welcome the dark nights of the soul with amens. There is grace and beauty and healing in all of it.

For you are on the road to blessed reassurance. There, you will meet your fears. Some will be etched in the faces of family, friends and lovers. Others will appear as dried-up dreams oozing doubt and regret. They may show up disguised as setbacks and disappointments. As dizzying as it may all seem, do not lose your grounding. These experiences are the most bountiful blessings of all!

On the road to blessed reassurance, you will meet your maker. You will come to know, in the words of John from the Holy Bible, "greater is he that is in you, than he that is in the world." Be still and know that you are standing on bedrock! Nothing can shake your foundation when you are turning within, resting in God, trusting in love and dwelling in the Presence.

Be still and know that you are made of fiery filament! Your dreams illumine the sky. You have the power to launch a billion satellites and the capacity to pacify a restless world.

Be still and know that you are not alone! Accompanying you and indwelling you is the Almighty Spirit! It never tires of revealing Its love as It whispers in your ear, *"You are my beloved, in whom I am well pleased."* Then, buoyed by this love, you will sway back and forth effortlessly with each earth-shaking change that comes your way. And your movements will become a kinetic dance with the Divine.

PEAK
SPEAK

I move in perfect harmony with God and all of life!
Nothing fazes me when I am filled with praise!

77

The Business of Being

I$_T$'S NOT WHAT, WHEN, WHERE OR HOW—these are not your business. The universe will attend to such matters. Instead it's all about the *who*. *Who* will you be? *Who* are you going to show up as this day? Will you show up as sons and daughters of the Most High, resplendent in your glory? Will you take up your bed, walk and sashay? Will you command mountains to move, expecting them to do exactly that, not some day but right now?

Everything is possible if you are courageous enough, surrendered enough, to wear the sparkling crown of your own divinity. You have at your disposal a treasure trove of gifts to mine and excavate. You are made of starry stuff. The constellations configure and bow to your majesty. The sun and the moon stepped aside to make way for your entrance when you were incarnated. They recognize you and are grateful for your appearance on the planet at this time. You are so needed, this is so readily apparent. But will you remember who you are, truly?

There is a reason and a season and a purpose for your life—and it is quite simple. You are here to be. The busyness and harried getting and spending are a distraction from the truth of it all. Be regal. Be in reverence. Be irreverent. Be open. Be available. Be light. Be magnificence. Be fearless. Be laughter. Be forgiveness. Be peace. Be life. Be love. Be the beloved.

Who you are is so much more significant than what is going to happen, when something is happening, why something is happening, or how something is happening. The Infinite Intelligence that thought to create you knows the what, the when, the why and the how. Revel in *who* you are. Trust.

PEAK
SPEAK

I bask in the glory and the magnificence of all that I am! I am here for God and for grace and for good!

Remember and Release

LET GO OF ALL THE MEMORIES that anchor you in regret. There is no heart space for this pain. There is no room for faithlessness and fear. There is too much crowding your thinking when that which in the end amounts to nothing is clamoring for your attention. As if to say, "Feed me. Stoke me. Give me life." No more! Bloated, misshapen dreams festering in the dregs of inhumanity have nowhere to go. Release them. Cut off their lifeline and banish them forever.

Together we can transmute the being*mess* into being*ness*. No efforting is needed, only a willingness to surrender. Give up thinking you have to *do* anything, say anything, know anything. Give up hoping and making and forcing.

Just breathe, just be. There is a stillness now, a fluidity, a phenomenal surrendering. Calm waves absorbing every tear you have ever shed now have permission to wash over you, for you have stood in your majesty and grace, and granted them permission to do so. How magnificent it is to command your fears to yield to the life force within you, to the Spirit that is you! And yield they must! There is no other way. Even as you walk in beauty like the night, rooting your dervish-like brainwaves into holy thinking, you soar. You are grounded in limitless awareness as you dare to fly into the sun, knowing that there is no way your wings will melt.

You are so much bigger than this—this thing that seems to have you in its grip. But it has no power over you. Relish the victory. Your little self has seen your shadow. It looms large and is filled with enough light to illuminate the heavens.

PEAK SPEAK

I am able to transcend any situation and any erroneous thought through sheer Spirit! Gratefully and gracefully I move from beingmess to beingness with love, light and delight!

When Your Soul Says Yes

NOW IS THE TIME TO RELEASE everything that with slow resolve has deterred you from bringing forth your innate power and grace—but still longs to flower through your aching bones. Now is the time to recall anguished renunciations and lingering doubts, and to put them to rest. There is no longer a need to delve into the sordid or the sorrow, you need not feign indifference. It is time to bask in the makings of you. It is time to revel in the activation of your soul. It is time to say yes!

Say yes to joy and embrace the surprises embedded in every moment. Say yes to your simmering dreams and call out your shadow from behind the trees. Say yes to delight and let it ravish you until your cup overflows with laughter. You can even say yes to your fears: "I see you, I thank you and I embrace you with love." Fears can't help but dissolve once they are acknowledged and blessed. They will wither on the vine, loosen their grip and wash up on the shores of your surrender.

When your soul says yes, earthquakes shake you down to your roots and volcanoes erupt to spew hope and resolve. When your soul says yes, you are able to leapfrog through galaxies and perform pirouettes through rainbows. When your soul says yes, you dare to gaze into the unknown and come to realize that you are known. Every star flickers for you, every grain of sand lives to have you caress it. The ground beneath you becomes solid. Your stance is firm. When your soul says yes, improbabilities take on the shape of realities. You remember that you are alive and that all is well. Say yes to your soul and be made whole. Be free!

PEAK
SPEAK

When I say yes to my soul I am able to rejoice in the splendor of me. Life flows because I am in the flow!

The Fire This Time

IN THE MIDST OF THE FIRE, claim your purification, your edification, your transformation. The holy wholeness of your being welcomes being put through the flames of alchemy. You may resist at first, but no matter. Chemicalization begets a christening of the highest order: You will begin to walk and talk anew. You are a new being— a creature no longer made out of clay but one soldered from the fiery songs of innocence and experience.

Like lava you will ooze and bubble over towers of humanity as you fossilize and crystallize errant thoughts and ways of being. You are the disruptor and the eruption. You are the volcano and its ashes. There will be nothing left for you to do but to build again, to create again, to pour yourself into everything you see, do and are becoming.

But this time you will know to let your love, and not your fear, take root. In the fire this time, you will no longer desire to mold others into your image, forcing

All thought, all desires,
That are under the sun,
Are one with their fires,
As we also are one.

RUDYARD KIPLING

them to adopt your thoughts and beliefs about the world. You will only desire to watch their phoenixes rise from smoke and ashes.

This is the dawning of a new era. This is an age of great transmutation and clarification. You will no longer determine success by the number of things you have coveted and then acquired. Instead you will allow your heart to make its own calculations. How often did I rest in silence when I wanted to lash out, disagree, contest and decry? How many times did I allow instead of resist, fully aware that there is nothing to fight? There is only the steadfast surrendering of will to make way for The Way—greater love, peace, flow, abundance, communion, alignment, harmony and clarity.

PEAK
SPEAK

I open my heart to a greater love!
I open my heart to a fiery resolve to
transmute, transform and transcend!

We Are the Light

IN TIMES OF TROUBLE MOTHER MARY'S whispers to "let it be" can go unheard. Fear can be deafening. But because we are here for one another, we declare to everyone we meet, "I am a place of healing for your rage and your sorrow when you can feel nothing else. I come for you bearing glad tidings of joy, and gifts of peace and wholeness I place at your feet. Thank you for being born so that I can remember my own splendor."

Let's be about the universe's business of revealing the glory in each and every one of us. We are here to shine and sanctify the holy places within our hearts, our minds, our souls, our bones, our muscles. We are here to bring blood, sweat and tears of jubilation to the forefront of our consciousness so that we can heal and be healed. We are here for one another, regardless of race, creed or color; religious denomination or political beliefs; sexual orientation or species. We are here, we are here, we are here!

Lightworkers, unite! We are the source of indomitable, all-powerful energy. We have the ability to harness this energy and channel it into expansive, kinetic love for even those we denigrate and believe we hate.

We come to one another with compassion and kindness. We forgive ourselves for believing that we are not humane enough or loving enough to extend the olive branch of peace, when we believe we alone wear the cloak of correctness. Instead we are courageous enough to remove this garment—and all other insecurity blankets—and allow what is truly real to be visible for all to see: our selfless humanity. Then, we each wave the white flag of pure consciousness and drape it on a table upon which we break bread together.

PEAK
SPEAK

I am the light! I shine brightly so that I can be a place of healing and transformation for the planet!

Against All Odds

BREATHE. STAY YOUR FEARS. TRUST. You are one with all there is. There is no need to fret when you are claiming your power, your fortitude, your grace. You remember: How you are held and attended to by the Presence, hand and foot, heart and soul. How you always triumph despite seemingly insurmountable odds. How you part the seas and raise up mountains. How you rise and shine and give God the glory simply by inhaling and exhaling. You are a resplendent reimagining and reenactment of the universe bursting into creation. You are an integral part of the Ineffable. Because you exist, all of life unfolds with a natural rhythm.

Breathe. Stay your fears. Trust. Be grateful. There is so much to be thankful for right now. Consider the dynamism in and all around us. Consider the lilies, the roses *and* the thorns. Everything serves a purpose. You can let go of all the worry. You are boundless.

Breathe. Stay your fears. Trust. Be in the zen. You are meant to live a grace-filled life. Go fearlessly, go prayerfully. Whether erect or on bended knee, you are always in prayer mode, for every thought is a prayer and every action, a manifestation of that prayer. You are not merely in your element, you *are* the elements: Rain, snow, sun and fire. Light doesn't begin to tell the story of your glow and your flow. Morning leaves glisten with the dew of you—your brio, your pizzazz, your way of expressing the mystery and the majesty.

You appear to be on the verge of something magnificent, but the truth is, it is already happening. Whatever your heart seeks, it is happening now. Allow gratitude to flood your every cell. Be in thanksgiving for your life. Be in thanksgiving for all of life. This is it. That is all.

PEAK
SPEAK

I am grateful for the roses and for the thorns, for the blessings and for the sorrows. I am enriched by every experience. I know God for myself.

Fearless Love

DO NOT BE LIMITED BY WHAT YOU SEE. Instead, be inspired by the possibilities beckoning you to gather in quiet repose and summon all of life to join in a chorus of dynamic cohesion. We are here to step into a greater awareness of our innate power. We are here to channel this power—a lavish, regenerative love—into food, shelter, safety, wholeness and happiness. For everyone, not just for one particular individual or sex or race or species. We are here to create, manifest and heal. This is the reason for living, this is the sole soul purpose.

Once we recognize the ties that bind us to one another, we honor these bonds by making it our soul's purpose to find ways to further cement them. We accomplish this by eschewing the false prophets of profit and endeavoring to become saviors for grace. We channel all of our energy into devising heightened ways of sharing, loving, being.

Wheresoever you go, go with all your heart.

ATTRIBUTED TO CONFUCIUS

We remember that we are not only our brothers' and sisters' keepers, but that as stewards of the planet we bear responsibility for its very survival. Instead of building weapons of mass destruction, we manufacture tools of conscious, inspired healing. Instead of projecting hate, we put aside our fears, recognizing they are only illusions—ghosts of a self we transcended long ago. We render them extinct by following our natural instinct to love.

In order to become brave enough to accept this mandate, we must first address our fears with the fierce tenderness of a lover: "I embrace you with all of my heart, love and light. I forgive myself for ever doubting I was enough, and for thinking I had to prove I was worthy. I thank you for showing me where I needed to be more loving with myself. Bless you."

PEAK SPEAK

I trust myself and my connection to all of life!
Love outshines fear in any and all circumstances.
I am ready to go about my soul's business!

Go Directly to Jubilee

KNOW THIS MUCH: You may lay down your weapons of anger and fear, and start playing your heartstrings. You may strip away the tattered garments of your former selves and let them collapse in a heap at your feet. Instead, drape yourselves in coats of many colors stitched together with the threads of your spiritual practices. You have prayed and meditated and visioned. You have stood at the door and knocked, and perhaps you are still knocking.

Just be mindful that whatever answers may not behave gently. The time for gentle discourse and polite conversation has passed. No more half-hearted mantras and reserved prayers. No more standing still when you are meant to move forward. No more directionless, frantic motion when you are meant to be still.

You see, Spirit wants to hurl you full throttle into the life you have always envisioned for yourself! It wants

We can come to God
Dressed for Dancing
Or,
Be carried on a stretcher
To God's Ward.

HAFIZ

to knock you to your knees—not in prayers of supplication, but in praise songs of grace and gratitude. You are meant to speak in tongues, bypassing decipherable language so that you go directly to jubilee. You are destined to raise the dead dreams languishing in your heart. Play your harps! This thing called Infinite Glory Be seeks to have full dominion over your every thing. It longs to pour Itself into you so that you are floating on pure dynamic energy and swimming in serenity.

Then, when you grow tired of rationalizing and resisting, when you are truly surrendered, It wants to swoop down from the altar of your Most High Selves, and wrap you in rainbows. The spectrum of colors now available to you is astonishing. Drink them in so that you are on fire for God and for your very life.

PEAK
SPEAK

I radiate bold new hues on the color wheel of life.
My light is a beneficial beacon everywhere
I shine—and I shine everywhere!

TERRAIN OF
GESTATION

Valley

LANDSCAPE OF SOLACE

When We Are Seeking Peace

Riverbank

LANDSCAPE OF ANTICIPATION

When We're Contemplating Jumping In

Garden

LANDSCAPE OF BIRTH

When We Are Ready to Flower

You Are Already There

THERE IS NO BRIDGE to build or fork in the road to take you to your destination. Crumbled passageways may have left pebbles in your shoes and splinters in your soul, but you have arrived. You see, winding courses are for sauntering and discerning, pondering and praising. And a maze becomes the ultimate plaything: At times you may think there is no way out, but the way out is the way into the depths of you. You trudge right into your very own synapses and heart muscles, firing up tender feelings and emotions. The sticky residue of a hurt serves as your guide to a more expanded you, a more vitalized you, a more available you.

Do you seek love, peace, light and more love? They await your rediscovery for they are already resting, like unearthed totems, in the hallowed grounds of your being. To excavate them is to remember: You remember to replace the grit with gratitude. You recall how to breathe a real breath—a deep, cleansing inhalation followed by an exhalation that yields the clarity and peace you desire. If you were to revel in the glory of you, you couldn't help but glow, producing an inimitable light. The love that you desire would immediately flood your awareness and eternal life would seek you out. It would regard you as a hospitable host for all the good it longs to lavish upon you. Then, you would be complete.

Welcome to the best you to have ever graced the planet. You have arrived at the door of your awakening and all you need to do is turn the key. Then, step across the threshold of your unbelief and claim the revitalization of your majesty. You are already there and the angels sing praises in your name. You are welcome.

PEAK
SPEAK

I welcome and relish the next chapter of my amazing existence! I am love, peace, light and life! Life is so good!

Just Breathe

Dear Beloved,

Perhaps you have forgotten. Now you may remember. Attune your heart to my syncopation. Focus all of your attention on me. When the world begins to spin you will remain in balance, graceful enough to dance on the point of a needle—and the only thing to fall away will be that which you no longer need. You are on solid ground.

Perhaps you have forgotten to breathe. Remember that in between each inhalation and exhalation, I am there. In between the doubt and the certainty, I am there. In between longing and manifestation, I am there. In between the singing of the note and the hearing of the note, I am there. In every blade of grass, in every ray of light, in solemn contemplation, in sublime ridiculousness, in frenzied motion, in resignation, in stagnation. I. Am. Here.

Just breathe. I live in you. I nurtured you in the womb, suckled when you suckled, then carried you across vast deserts of indecision, fear, worry and denial. Your footprints are etched in my footprints.

I was also there for the mirages, the milk and the honey. I paved the landscape with gold, brick by brick. I helped you build altars in my name, then sanctified the hallowed spaces in your body temple, atom by atom. I launched rockets into the atmosphere to fire up your senses and your sensibilities. I planted trees in your honor so that you would be fertile in your imagination and abundant in your thoughts about what is possible.

Good God, how we used to create! And there is more to manifest. I have always been here for you. There is no place I would rather be because there is no other place to be. I am with you. I live in you. Remember, just breathe.

Love,

God In You and As You

PEAK SPEAK

I see and am seen by the One. I rejoice in God and God rejoices in me. God is all there is. Truly!

Faith of Our Fathers and Mothers

TAP INTO THE RESERVOIR of soul-edifying recompense aggregated by those who have come before you. Make no mistake, you have been born into a lineage of tender, loving possibility. Now you can tend to your own tenacity. The roads before you stretch ahead of you beyond reckoning, promising all manner of reconciliation. And because this is so, all of your dreams take flight and bask in golden light should you give voice to them. They dance, they flutter, they exhale.

Remember, the fruits of both your labor and your languor are temptingly good—and equally beneficial. When you exert, pursue and strive, you generate, but it is within the breadth of release that you truly create. Then you are free to reveal your bravado and grace, for you have been liberated from the bondage of insecurity, fear and self-judgment.

Those who have come before you act as sentries: They prepare the way for your arrival on the planet, support the dance that is your life, and help orchestrate your return into the ether, into All That Is and All That Shall Ever Be. You are never alone. The ancestors are always spinning webs of feather-light majesty to support you. You can jump uninhibited upon them knowing that wherever you land, you will be catapulted into glory yet again.

There is no end to the love field you have inherited. You can run haphazardly toward what you perceive to be the edge, only to encounter yet another expanse—an unfamiliar landscape with its unique climate and terrain. There is no boundary that can contain you, no matter how much you push against it. The ancestors have planted and tilled the soil of your consciousness. Sometimes they whisper, sometimes they bellow. They await your acceptance, they await your mighty yes.

PEAK SPEAK

**I have the faith to believe and receive!
I am guided and I am loved!**

Yours, Eternally

Dear Beloved,

I wait. And I will continue to wait for you to awaken unto me and realize that I am here and I have always been here. I am here for you and as you, with you and in you.

You, who have gotten down on your knees, gazed up into the heavens, crossed your heart and fingered prayer beads in supplication, in meditation, in contemplation and sometimes in deep frustration.

At other times, I have observed you in joy, in silence, in reverence—shouting, praising, dancing. You have revealed the depth of your humanity and I have been there each and every step, jump and leap of the way. I have marveled at your resilience and your longing to know me, even when you believe I am pulling a disappearing act. Truly, you are made in my image. I gaze at you tenderly.

Me, for whom you have built majestic temples. Me, who longs to be your all 'n all, the only thing you live for.

Where healing waters flow
Do thou my footsteps lead.
My heart is aching so;
Thy gracious balm I need.

PAUL LAURENCE DUNBAR

Me, who has been so misunderstood: You have feared me, misinterpreted me and falsely thought there were things I needed you to do in order to prove you loved me. I needed no such evidence; I only wanted you to come willingly. I wanted you to learn these things for yourself, freely and without guilt or hair shirts or penance. For yielding leads to understanding. I knew that eventually you would come to realize just how much you mean to me.

We, the union that cannot help but exist, for it is together that we walk through the valley of the light of eternality. It is together that we love, we rejoice, we create. I wait for you for eternity. Eternally you. Eternally me. Eternally we.

Love,

God In You and As You

PEAK SPEAK

I come alive when I recognize and accept the interconnectedness that binds me to Spirit. I am here for God—and God is here for me.

Bring the Party

YOUR POWER IS IMMEASURABLE, boundless and beatific. Step right up, move past the conditions and concerns of your life, and take your place on the grand stage. You are charged with the life-affirming task of acting out the scenes, designing the sets, directing the action and choreographing the movements. This is *your* production.

Attune to your inner compass and embark on a new course. Well-trodden trails can no longer carry you or bear your weight. You are so much bigger than you ever were. Sense the vast opportunities summoning you into a new dimension. It's a brave new world, indeed. Revolutionize your thinking. You need not brandish a sword. Your words of love and manifestation cut through the rhetoric of mediocrity, soothing and healing festering wounds.

Honor and obey your soul's summoning of the real you—the essence that is you and longs to embrace you.

> *The universe is change;*
> *our life is what our thoughts make it.*
>
> **MARCUS AURELIUS**

It seeks to penetrate the density that is your humanness and catapult you into a new awareness. The glass isn't either half full or half empty; it's always full. You are not a spiritual being having a human experience; you are Spirit embracing humanity, and humanity embracing Spirit, all at the same time. Joy doesn't just come in the morning; it's here, *now*, available to you, *now*.

Those battles waging inside of you? Those rages that spill over into your lives creating headlines and wars? Banish them with grace and gratitude. Quiet them by giving them room to breathe. Yes, periodically they may clamor to regain your attention. Speak compassionately to them and bless them for all they have taught you. Then, be on your way. All of life is at your loving, affirming command. You get to *bring* the party and *be* the party. It all begins with you.

I am the creator of all that I see, think and feel. I bring the love, I bring the peace, I bring the party!

Valley

Alignment and Alchemy

Dear Beloved,

I am always communing with you, in all ways, at all times. There is not a veil I cannot breeze through, a false belief I cannot pierce, an illusion I cannot melt, in order to reach the tendermost parts of your being. And when I can cup your perception of separation from me and fling it into the heavens, thereby creating a shooting star, I am in a state of rapturous delight.

I delight in you as I rejoice in our re-alignment and our re-emerging and our re-remembering. Bit by bit, bone by bone, you come into balance. We harmonize so that we are one note ringing into eternity. There is nothing we cannot do, create and be! That cure, that jump shot, that monument ... it's all not only possible, it is already done. We become the miracle and then the matter.

The miracle happens when you yield to your divinity and have the vision to birth what is already rightfully yours. It is written that you are the sons and daughters of

*Every valley shall be exalted,
and every mountain and hill shall be made low:
and the crooked shall be made straight,
and the rough places plain*

ISAIAH 40:4

the Most High. What if you were to truly believe that you are in fact the Most High, and that it is your destiny to birth more life in all of its grandeur?

Then, you would realize that every sojourn is a return to love, and that every repudiation of me and consequently your own indisputable holiness, is a plea for balance. Every hurtful word becomes an ode to joy and forgiveness. There is alchemy in the tawdriest of transgressions. You need only remember to love in the midst of it all. We can love it all into nothingness so that the only thing you perceive is our alignment and our union and communion. I am here.

Love,

God in You and As You

PEAK SPEAK

When I choose to see who and whose I truly am, life happens, love happens! I am an unstoppable force for love, alchemy and radical healing!

In Your Finest Hour

Dear Beloved,

How I have longed for this opportunity to come heart-to-heart with you.

You've been expecting me, this I know. For I have already sent many signs of our deep connection: When you marvel at the rain and rainbows, you are expressing gratitude for our dynamic union. When you laugh heartily or clasp the hand of the dying, you honor our integrated nature. As you take each breath, you pay homage to me. Thank you!

Some of you, however, have come to believe that I stand idly by, oblivious to your needs. You hold onto the notion that I never existed, that I am some sort of a phantom, or that I have fallen asleep at the wheel.

You cling to the idea that I am a slumbering giant who can only be roused out of its sleep when a tsunami of tears floods the earth. Then and only then do I show up, my cape flapping behind me in the wind like a superhero.

The feeling remains that God
is on the journey, too.

ATTRIBUTED TO SAINT TERESA OF ÁVILA

Or perhaps you spend your time pondering the existential question of the ages: If God truly does exist, why then is there so much suffering in the world? You don't really believe in me.

But the soul-shattering truth I have attempted to show you—through your relationships with one another and through the master teachers I have appointed to excavate the burial grounds of your soul for traces of life—is that I do not exist if you deny me and refuse to see me in everything. For I am nothing without you!

Will you see me? I am right here. In your finest hour, you will come to know this and I will be more real than anything you can perceive with your five senses.

Love,

God In You and As You

PEAK
SPEAK

I am the face of God.
I see God everywhere I go.
This, I believe.

Clarion Call

Within the note within the note within the note is where you can be free. There, you can chase down your inner demons, rip off their masks and plant a kiss of forgiveness on their ravaged lips and cheeks, all the while singing of promise and praise. There, you can finally hear soul-shifting truth. Not only will it set you free, it will also liberate others imprisoned by their own personal fears.

Listen for the tones of your temerity: they are markedly hollow, which is a good thing. There is no density to penetrate, to bear down upon, to infiltrate and alchemize. Instead, everything is as light as whispering air and as ephemeral as beams bouncing off a cascading waterfall.

Frank, confrontational talk is for the timid, the fearful, the uninitiated. The challenge is to allow the voice of reason to soothe your fears with tender tones: "There, there, we've got you. Life is good. All the time." Especially when things would suggest otherwise.

All things respond to the call of rejoicing;
all things gather where life is a song.

CHRISTIAN D. LARSON

Now you can invite in the revelry. Now you can hear the note within the note within the note within the note. It sounds like joy and laughter and the tuning of heartstrings. It sounds like resonance itself. There is no place, no thought, no idea, where you are not strumming along to the symphony only your soul was created to play.

Now you can canvass the landscapes of your indecisiveness and plant seeds of courteous, yielding majesty. It is not your rootedness that will propel you forward in your life, though certainly with this foundation, you are off and running towards greater vistas and higher summits. Instead, it is your flexibility, your beginner's mind-meld with the omniscient Presence that brought you to where you are in the first place, that will show you the way to go every time. Listen.

PEAK
SPEAK

I speak to my inner child with loving tones.
I address my being with a gentle knowing that is
always inviting, always kind. I only hear love.

You Have Been Summoned

Dear Beloved,

I am summoning you to a dance with the Divine. Take my hand! I will lead you and guide you every step of the way. What song wants to be plucked from your heart-strings? What new thought is straining the fibers of your synapses, eager to take form? What great awakening is rattling the cages of your pent-up frustrations in the hope that if enough shaking, rattling and rolling transpires within your soul, an eruption will happen? Smoke and fire and molten lava will ooze down upon you and bake you into a brand new fiery being. You will fear nothing, and you will love everything and everyone!

I am summoning you to a meeting with your heart, for it is there that you will find me. Surely, you have heard me knocking at the door of your despair! Some of you have falsely thought that I have been either too busy or too angered by you. You may have felt abandoned, dislocated, discombobulated. In those times, I have gently

*Thou hast made us for Thee,
and the heart knows no rest
until it rests in Thee.*

SAINT AUGUSTINE

wrapped myself around you then squeezed you so tightly, you thought you couldn't breathe. That's because I was breathing you.

I am summoning you to a feast of thanksgiving! I have been preparing for our reunion—and it is now. Now that you have had the wisdom to see that truly we are one. Now that you have harnessed your intrinsic powers and chosen to bless your own being, and others, too. Now that you know you can always commune with me through a prayer, a meditation, a whisper, a sigh. Now that you have come to know yourself, to forgive yourself, to love yourself. Now that you are ready. Please sit at the table and break bread with me. You will be fed.

Love,

God In You and As You

PEAK SPEAK

I am grateful for the undeniably effervescent Essence and Presence living Its life as me. I honor God when I honor myself; when I honor myself, I honor God.

In God's Hands

REJOICE, NOW. SING, NOW. DANCE, NOW. Through stormy nights laden with heavy burdens and tears. Through desert storms and thunderous, rolling clouds. Through tempestuous terrains and moods swinging with the velocity of tornadoes. It is incumbent upon you— whoever you think you are, wherever you are, whatever you have done and whatever you believe has been done to you—to attune your heart to the pulse of pregnant possibility and remember: You've got this.

Let these words wash over you. Let these words take you down to the depths of the Nitty Gritty, into the Abyss of the Absolute and up and out again into the Far and Wide. Beyond fear, worry, doubt and denial. You've. Got. This.

And here is why: Because God's got *you*! In Its hands, in Its embrace, in Its grace and in Its love, It's got you. Wrapped up in rainbows, aloft in blue skies, nestled in fertile soil, awash in brilliant light. Yes, you are trans-figured, simply because It gets you. It understands your tendencies and your idiosyncrasies, your ways of being and doing, your ways of glowing and growing.

Now, breathe this in: You are known and recognized by the Our Father Who Art in Heaven and On Earth Presence. You are birthed by the Our Mother Who Art in Heaven and On Earth beingness. Not just at conception and arrival, but in the living as you contemplate survival. In every moment you are being reborn. You lead a royal existence. There is no way in heaven you could ever forsake your crown because you are sons and daughters of the Most High. You are the anointed ones. The world longs to touch the hem of your garment. Rejoice, because everything—both animate and inanimate—is declaring with a mighty voice, *"We've got this. Oh yes, we do!"*

PEAK SPEAK

I allow God's love to anchor me and to lift me up!
God speaks through me; I speak through God!

There is Light in the Tunnel

Dear Beloved,

I am that I am and all that I am, and all that you are—and all that we forever shall be. This much is true: I have no need of distinguishing where I end and you begin, or where you end and I begin, because there is only our inextricable existence. We are bound up in one another.

I cannot help but respond to your every prayer and every plea, your every tear and every tantrum. I am a most indulgent Mother-Father-God, so bring it on! Your disavowals of me do not anger me or frustrate me. They make me want to prove you whole instead of wrong, holy instead of hollow. They inspire me to bathe you in my love-light even more. I am a most ardent suitor. Your rebuffs could never dissuade me from seeing your glory.

You see, I will not hold back my grace, whether real or perceived, under any circumstances. You can sense me in the bowels of the most heart-shattering catastrophes and in the agony of the most piercing cries. I am the hurdle

*And the light shineth in darkness;
and the darkness comprehended it not.*

JOHN 1:5

over the most dire obstacles. I will catapult you into clearer vision, understanding and compassion for yourself and for others. I will see you through. Healing and hope wait for no one. They come fully unleashed, overcoming faithlessness and forgetfulness. They pierce the veils of illusion and disillusionment. They will not be hampered by tunnel vision or deterred by despair.

Light will not force you to hold your applause until the end of the performance. It seeks its bows in the overture and in every act, in the finale and in the encore. There is light in the tunnel. I am that light. See me now.

Love,

God In You and As You

PEAK
SPEAK

Wherever I am, whatever I am growing through, I embrace the light. God is right where I am, now and always!

117

A Life is God Writ Large

To FOCUS ONE'S GAZE UPON an inner vision is to surrender and let God be God. Grace does the seeing. The heart does the hearing. And God, always God, bestows the rhymes and the rhythms, the allusions and the allegories, the imagery and the imagination.

When you surrender, God will let it flow—whether it's the words onto the page or a vision for your life. Your inner resolve can't help but yield guidance, awareness and blessed reassurance.

You see, a blank page is never actually empty when one is collaborating with the Divine. Its emptiness heralds a promise: There will be creativity and beauty and moments of transcendent revelry. There will be poetry and psalms and poetry slams—and yes, you will remember and you will surrender.

A life yearning to be lived out loud never goes unfulfilled when you allow God to breathe into you, to inhabit your every thought, to fill up your senses, to guide your steps, to whisper sweet everythings into your ear, to be your compass, to both whet and satiate your appetite, to meet your every need, to be your guiding light as well as the love of your life—to let it be.

Now, in this reverential moment, imagine words dancing above an empty page. What inner vision longs to take shape in your life right now? How will you allow God to breathe life into that vision? How will you co-create with Spirit this vision so that it can transition from your inner world, embody your being, then take hold in the world at large? How will you string together letters and words, ideas and inspiration, and hopes and dreams, so that they become your Word with a capital W? And so it is written.

PEAK SPEAK

My life is the manifestation of my word, aspirations and inner visions coming together in a most dynamic way. I choose to co-create with God every day in every way.

The Truth of You

It IS TIME TO GET REAL and to see the splendor in every moment. It is time to see the indisputable truth of you—your beauty, your sweetness, your formidable nature. It is time to bow down before your inner mystic and to honor It by listening to the notes that were created just for you. They resonate with your own particular rhythm. It is time to obey the call of your soul's contract and shine like the original blessing that you are. The constellations require your light.

Get real and know your truth. There is nothing you cannot achieve when you choose to practice the Presence. There is no dream left deferred when you remember you are the creator as well as the co-creator, the genius, the Ineffable and the majesty. You chose this time, this place, this incarnation.

Get real and heal yourself of the mistaken belief that you should be doing something other than what you are doing right now. There are no rest stops on the journey. Every station is a gateway to your next you.

> *Man flows at once to God when*
> *the channel of purity is open.*
>
> **HENRY DAVID THOREAU**

You can't make a false move. Life is calling you forth and wants for you what is in your heart—so inhabit your life.

Trust in your inner knower, power and grace. Be still so that you can distinguish Its love from your fear, Its tenderness from your judgment. It lives to serve you and honor you. It thrives when you surrender to Its blessings.

Dive in so that you wade into unchartered territories of consciousness. Hold onto your awareness of your divinity, even when quicksand threatens to smother your faith. Fasten your hopes to what is real. God, only God. Always God. You are the rapture as old ways of being evolve into new and dynamic expressions. You are glory itself.

PEAK
SPEAK

When I realize my realness, my power and my truth, I am unstoppable. I know why I am here!

All Systems Go

Dear Beloved,

You have huddled in the shadows. You have held back your power. You have denied your own divinity, waiting on some false god to anoint your head with oil. No more! No longer can you hide. There are too many stumbling around in darkness, unaware that there is light in the tunnel. There are too many who have forgotten.

Here is what I have come to remind you. We're in this love together and if you plant a flower, you grow a pearl. I speak to you through song and dance, through rainbows and meteor showers. I show up as your reflection. I embrace you now—for who you are now—whether you rest in silence or rage with all the passion and fury of a hurricane. I accept you for who you are. I love you as you are.

I am your God. I create you in my image, and you create me in yours. I have dallied and dawdled, thinking that you will invite me to dance with you. How I long to take the lead and guide you over those crooked paths, *for I know where the bumps and hurdles lie. I can ferry you over bridges spanning troubled waters. I can help you mount onto angel wings that carry you high above any semblances of imperfection or wrongness.*

I am your God. I know that together we have so much to create.

I am your God. I relish every opportunity we spend together in the silence.

I am your God. I am birthing you in every nanosecond—and you are birthing me. You get to view the world through my eyes. You get to marvel at all that is, just as I do. Ours is the holiest of unions. It is eternal, it is now.

Love,

God In You and As You

PEAK
SPEAK

I am infused with the Holy Spirit! I am ready for lift-off! It's all good and all grace from now through eternity!

Coming Attractions

Because THERE IS NO TIME, and because now is the time, there is nothing that has not already happened in the mind of God. The miracle is to glimpse it—that which your soul wishes to call forth, even that which is so grand your mind cannot grasp it—in the here and now. See it anyway, for if you can dream it, you can realize it by kneading it with faith and trust: That soul-alchemizing, soul-edifying relationship. That perfect job or career, home or holy sanctuary. It's all visible now in the invisible.

But you have to believe it to see it. You have to see it to reveal it. And here's how: Gently close your eyes. Now, inhale and exhale slowly repeatedly until you sense that something magnanimous and magnificent is breathing you. Stroll down by the riverside that appears in your mind's eye. If you look out beyond life's sometimes choppy waters, you will notice gossamer figures dancing in your honor. They are named Promise and Principle.

You see things; you say, "Why?"
But I dream things that never were;
and I say, "Why not?"

GEORGE BERNARD SHAW

They are called Light and We've Got This. They come to remind you that your dreams are taking shape—dreams that no longer haunt you but inspire you.

The coming attractions reveal themselves through all of the love and the beauty, through all of the joy and the song. You've seen the signs pointing the way. You can detect them in the grace of this day. When everything seemed to go awry, there was a shift. Perhaps someone shared with you a wonder and you realized that their blessings were also yours to be had. You shifted from rehash to revelation instantaneously, marveling at your own largesse. You were aware enough to be good and kind to yourself.

What will you claim for yourself this day? What will you give thanks for *now*?

PEAK
SPEAK

My very life is a preview of all the good seeking me! I claim all of my good now and I make good on my soul's promise to love God as me.

Beyond the Horizon

THERE MAY COME A TIME in your life when myopia sets in. You can see only what is right in front of you, and what is right in front of you are your concerns. These may loom large, like gigantic phantoms trailing you everywhere. They appear to be so real you actually believe you are awake.

During these times you may ask what seem like intelligent questions: What should I do?...What's going to happen?...Where am I headed?...You are tempted to get down on bended knee even if this isn't how you usually pray—as if doing so could induce God to bend Its will to your desires.

It's during these times, when we can no longer see clearly, that we must climb to a different altitude, longitude and latitude, and gaze upon our lives and the world at large. This new vantage point can be accessed through prayer, meditation and visioning laced with gratitude.

Once there, look at the horizon stretched out before you. There are ships at a distance sailing for grace-filled

> *When you get into a tight place, and everything goes against you till it seems as if you couldn't hold on a minute longer, never give up then, for that's just the place and time that the tide'll turn.*
>
> HARRIET BEECHER STOWE

shores. Tie your sorrows to the mast and store them in the hull. Then stand in wonder as all your cares are ferried to unknown territories that have never been discovered, not even by the great explorers. These lands are meant for only you to mine. They are inhabited by yea-sayers, not naysayers. Inevitably, you will adopt a different attitude, finally seeing the forest for the trees as you say yes to your deepest calling.

For when you allow your insecurities—those greedy goblins feeding on fear—to be transported to the outer banks of your consciousness, you will find buried treasure in your synapses, thoughts and words. You will speak in tongues, babbling coherently, eloquently, gratefully, "Thank you for showing me what is real—only God."

PEAK
SPEAK

I no longer believe the hype or even my sight. In God, the one truth, I trust. The trust shall set me free!

Riverbank

To Yield

Wander down roads that seem to carry you nowhere, for in the end you will arrive at a marvelous juncture. Veer off into unspoken, unnamed fears, for in them you will find the moral compass to direct you into true courage and surrender. Cross bridges that creak and sway, for you are being transported out of trepidation and into brave exploration and dynamic resolution. And when you find yourself at the riverbank, rejoice and let your soul enter deep contemplation. Answers await to be sifted and stirred.

Life has no time for fractured insurrection. Go bold! We are on a course of deliberate resurrection and true north lies beyond your doubts, beyond history and pattern, and far beyond indeterminate practice. You only appear to falter. Each fall from grace is actually a catapult into real living, real loving and real being. You come to know yourself and to realize that you are everything, and as such, everything is yours for the allowing. Resonance rules. Revelry takes over.

I'm not afraid of storms,
for I'm learning how to sail my ship.

LOUISA MAY ALCOTT

Every encounter becomes a reunion of sorts: You remember intention, purpose, fulfillment. And it feels so good! You are releasing the vestiges of a life you could not fully inhabit because you used to be afraid. And now there is only you—and more you! The love staring back at you when you look into the mirror is all consuming. It will not and cannot be extinguished. Within every molecule dancing in honor of your existence there is a potent chemicalization happening. You are peeling back the layers, grateful to rest in a space of not knowing. After all, you do not need to have the answers lined up just yet. Instead, you seek to be known, allowing awareness to penetrate. You are at the ready, yielding. Only then can life carry you.

PEAK
SPEAK

I release having to know and having to do.
I yield to the good in me, I yield to the glory of me!

The Big Reveal

Dear Beloved,

There will come a time when all of the pretensions and affectations will fall away. What your parents think, what your teachers taught you, even what you thought you thought, believed you believed, and felt you felt—all this will amount to nothing.

You will recall your opinions and your judgments, your ideals and your convictions, and you will understand just how wrong you were. Not because the other candidate or idea was more compelling. Not because the actual answer was yes when you thought it should have been no.

No, you will understand how misguided you were to have had an opinion in the first place, for this dynamic, expansive universe is too magnificent, too magnanimous, to be confined to a thought. Everything is transitory, fluid and flowing—and so are you! You get to create and recreate your vision for your life, your manifest destiny.

The quickest way to erect heaven on earth is to surrender it all. Give up all attachments and beliefs and free-float in the space between. Dive into the murkiness

Once I knew the depth where no hope was,
and darkness lay on the face of all things.
Then love came and set my soul free.

HELEN KELLER

of uncertainty. Feel free to suspend your belief in me! Go right ahead, I can take it. I have no need of your belief in me. But what I absolutely cannot bear are your little thoughts about your glorious selves.

And now, the big reveal! When you choose to stand naked before me, wearing only the garments of radical authenticity, you will be free to share with the world who you truly are. You will understand that you cannot be defined in any given moment or even a lifetime, for you are being refined eternally. You will see yourselves as I see you—utterly divine, spectacularly radiant and resplendently reborn.

Love,
God In You and As You

. I am ever-expanding in God and as God.
I surrender all!

Deepening

WHEN SWIMMING IN THICK murky waters one can reach out and grasp infinity. When skating on thin ice, one can grow wings and glide in the air. When dancing on the edge, one can jump into the void and make contact with solid ground.

In a state of trust, all things are possible. We grow by leaps and bounds, stretching the soul and contorting into fantastic shapes that are dizzying to imagine. A new creature is born, for an old one has been resurrected. We no longer thirst, for we see the ebb and the flow of the tides, and realize we are drowning in divinity. Our very souls lap up onto the shores of celestial grandeur.

To get to this place, we must surrender. Not the kind of surrender that comes embalmed in sighs waving white flags, as if to say, "I give up." No, this is the kind of surrender that lovingly gives. As in, "I give God the glory." Or "I give it up for Spirit and applaud the good that is already mine." We are grateful.

Spiritual practice makes perfection visible. We can see clearly. We see ourselves. And what a sight we are to behold! We look inward and glimpse the miracle that we are. From an idea, solid human expression. From the nothingness that is everything, a dynamic amalgam of love and spitfire. From an egg and a sperm, life!

It's been written we are each made in God's image. But we don't hail from an assembly line of incarnation. We each break the mold and become something as glorious as the original. There's nothing carbon copy about us. We are like none other. Holy unique. Wholly divine! Think on this the next time you feel yourself flailing and falling. You are actually deepening.

PEAK
SPEAK

I see beyond appearances and recognize that I am growing minute by minute as I expand into eternity!

The Grace in Surrender

THERE EXISTS A WAY OF LOVING AND BEING, a way of seeing and knowing, a way of revealing and reveling, that is yours for the asking and for the accepting. You do not have to wait until you have landed the perfect mate or job or home. You can have it all now—the blessings, the grace, the epiphanies, the joy, the peace, the light and the delight. All of your dreams await your manifestation. They long to emerge from the din of possibility into the dazzling flow of realization. They ache to propel you into the next dimension of your spiritual unfolding. They want to materialize before your very eyes so as to render gossamer images concrete, tangible, palpable— to make the invisible visible.

But how to immerse yourself in the real without falling prey to the unfathomable?

First, let go of the notion that you are navigating the waters of your life in a tugboat or cargo vessel. You are not bogged down by freight; you are immersed in faith!

Next, call out your aspirations from their perch atop wings of desire. Finally, thank your inspirations for igniting you from within.

You must decide. Are you willing to create and activate and flow, even as you are rooted? Are you willing to bend and dip, even as you stand erect in your truth? Surrender unto grace now! Grace will overcome your dictates and mandates. Grace will rise up and disarm your most outlandish fears and insecurities. Suddenly you realize there's no need to wield the sword and shield of expectation and desperation. You can let go and allow the inevitable Ineffable to take over and hold full sway. You are peace itself, you are love itself, you are life itself. All is well. Breathe.

PEAK SPEAK

I am so anchored in my faith I flow the way God flows and surrender unto my innate grace.

There Will Be Change

Dear Beloved,

I speak to you in all ways. I commune with you through the sun's rays and I illuminate your thoughts with moonbeams. I create a trajectory for your life in the pattern of stones skipping upon the waters. I guide your path with footprints in the sand and sky, and on the ocean floor. I massage your tender muscles and hurts with cascading leaves.

I share my love for you in the way I have designed the constellations. They are so brilliantly clustered, there is little space in between each speck of light; it's all one soothing blanket of illumination. And yet sometimes when you look up, all you can see is blackness. I am there, too, speaking to you in dulcet tones.

I am fond of uttering sweet nothings and savory everythings. These can be detected in the fluttering of a bird's wings, in the notes in between the notes, and in every motion, sensation, vibration and exclamation.

When you are asleep, I hold vigil at your bedside and whisper into your eyes and ears and fingertips and toes

*the only commandment that ever truly matters: Love and
Be Love.*

*I am all things. I am everywhere. And because I am
ever present, ever constant, everything else must change.
But I remain the glue. Embrace the stunning array of
possibilities splayed out before you in your seasons of
unknowns. Be pliable and let me do the shaping and the
molding. Avail yourself of the freshness of a new day,
a new year, a new thought, a brand new way of viewing
the world and the reflection peering back at you in the
mirror. I have brought you this far, I have planted your
feet where you are—for now—and I will carry you through
to a brand new you.*

Love,

God In You and As You

God guides me in both the known and the unknown
throughout my life. The Divine's messages penetrate my
soul and my purpose. I am exactly where I need to be!

A Time to Reap

IT IS TIME TO BRING in the sheaves. Rejoice as you harvest the fruits of your labor and your joy, of your sorrow and your surrender, for they have served you well. They open the gateways to deep transformation. They fortify you.

It is time to touch the hem of your own garment. You are draped in love. Love is woven into every fiber of your being. Each thread vibrates with potentiality and promise. You are the designer and the weaver, the needle and the thread. You pick the pattern and get to change it again and again. Alterations are essential and a given. Spirit knits and casts off so that you do not unravel. God is truly binding.

It is time to soar like the eagle for you are the eagle. You can fly into the blazing sun then dive deep into the ocean's depths without so much as a break in the breath. There is no altitude sickness when you are riding high on trust.

It is time to remove the boulders blocking your heart. Roll them away with a passion that could disintegrate the most hardened fears calcified after years of fortifying misplaced loyalties and hurts. Instead, fossilize your faith. Dig deep into the rich earth and excavate your forgotten dreams. Those rocks and specks of sand and clay are there to refine the ragged edges you didn't even know you had.

It is time to exit the lion's den. There are no more creatures to wrestle. All that needs to be slain is you—in the Spirit.

It is time to synthesize the music inside of you. Let the grace notes float into the atmosphere, resound like the music of the spheres.

Yes, it is time to walk on water for you are the Christ. Your very life beckons.

PEAK
SPEAK

In every new season of my life, I plant seeds of thanksgiving and harvest God's greater vision for my life.

Influx and Flow

STAND RIGHT WHERE YOU ARE NOW—whether your tears threaten to drown you, or whether you are simply wading in the waters of your own discontent and sorrow. Be still right now. Let the currents wash up against the shores of your unbelief. The tides, they follow your soular cycles. If you ebb, you will flow—and when you flow, you will be cleansed of anything and everything that no longer serves you.

It is time to trust. You are ready to gather streams of faith into a tsunami wave upon which you can surf. Soon you will ride a succession of delights that will carry you into your desires, into your destiny. You won't just crest the wave, you will dance and pirouette upon it. Flow is happening, and the influx of thoughts and insights, of epiphanies and triumphs, of wild abundance and daring creativity, is at hand. In fact, it is guaranteed: influx always follows flow. The more you surrender to the flow—that is, the less you are in resistance—the more easily you will be propelled into your most dynamic, most radiant self.

Remember, you are here, and you are here now for a unique divine purpose. It is your soul's intention to recall what exactly that is. Let your memories take you to a time when you were so very certain and your faith was unshakeable. When you were free enough to paint your rainbows with stripes and polka dots. Swaths of vibrant hues were too dull. Then, if you were hungry or tired, you cried. You allowed your emotions to surface without stoppering them so that you could move on to the next thought, the next thing. You knew that every condition was temporary and you held out for a fresh new moment. That moment is now. Embrace it. Flow.

PEAK SPEAK

I allow an influx of goodness and grace to carry me to higher ground! I am ready to flow and thrive!

Adventures in Consciousness

STOP. LOOK. LISTEN. To your heart, to the beating of a swallow's wings, to the flutter of a shimmering blade of grass as it sways in the wind. You are here, now—in the place where everything you have dreamed of is about to be realized in the palpable air of reckoning. All of your thoughts are coalescing. All of your beliefs are spiraling and then congealing. You are ready.

How does it feel to know that everything is unfolding exactly as you longed, beseeched, bargained and even borrowed? (Surely you remember those times you had so little trust you tapped into the faith of your ancestors. They weren't so long ago!)

You can forgive yourself for any doubts you may have had on the journey. Each one led you here. In fact, they conspired on your behalf for they knew that their gentle nudging—and their full-on assaults and somersaults—would catapult you to where you are now. All of the plateaus created a jigsaw puzzle of a ladder up, up and away into consciousness. Each ricochet ratcheted

*A bird is safe in its nest—but that is not
what its wings are made for.*

AMIT RAY

up your trust, your awareness, your purpose. Your misadventures all brought you here, to this fresh, new now.

There is only one thing left to do: surrender. Become so surrendered that you float in clouds of gracious consciousness. Be so free that in each split second your atoms playfully decide what form to take.

How easy it is to call forth what you want when your heart is leading the way! You know. You have always known that you would arrive at this place. What you determined through a plethora of experiences is the how: Would you allow the grit of your travails to overtake you—or would you invoke the high commandment to be pure in heart? Open your eyes and see God. This is a fresh new now.

PEAK
SPEAK

I am awakened! I am ready for my new life!
Bring on the blessings!

Gestation Mandate

As a brand new earth revolves around the sun and a brand new you is being called forth into being, begin to question not how or why or when—but *what*.

What has been gestating and now wishes to come to life within you, through you and as you? A child, a song, a testament, a revelation, a memory, a monument? What messages are your ancestors sending you in your dreams? What vision, inspired by a visitation of spirits, wants to spring forth into reality? What longs to rise up in you making your cup runneth over, irrigating barren wastelands—those places within you that you thought could never be revived?

Be still. Pray. Listen. Discern. Quell the fear through transcendent heart-seeing. That so-called problem is actually a call for high resolve! See beyond the ghost-like images of the human condition. They are merely figments of your separation, for true imagination isn't fractured or fake. It's other-worldly real.

Consider what vision-based reality is taking shape as you enter this new life-new you-new year cycle.

Instead of making resolutions, start a revolution! Be dauntless as you storm the castles of constriction and tear down the self-imposed barriers that up until now may have blocked your ascension from mortal to godhead. For this is your divine rightful inheritance, which no one—not even your fears—can deny you:

To bless and be blessed.

To command souls to free themselves by loving one another.

To imprint a declaration of life, liberty and the pursuit of unbridled happiness upon the hearts of all.

To satisfy the longing of your soul's forgotten hopes and aspirations.

To achieve greatness, to dream the impossible dream.

It's a new day, a new year, but more importantly, it's a new you. Be restored and renewed—and rejoice!

PEAK SPEAK

I am launching a revolution of evolution as I bring forth God's grandest vision for my life!

Garden

From Aha to Ta-da

IN PRECIOUS AHA MOMENTS suddenly we get it. We see in our mind's eye the magnificent gifts we are meant to deliver to the world. We remember the true nature of our being—our very essence is holy, glorious God-stuff. We arrive at a deeper understanding of why we are here. Then and only then do we truly open the gateways to eternality and rise into the bliss that is rightfully ours. We inherit the earth, the heavens, and everything in between. "Yes!" our souls pronounce. "And so it is."

But these times of insight often signify a beginning and are not necessarily meant to be the end result. There are even more remarkable moments in store for us and they, too, make up our divine rightful inheritance.

For the *aha* moment often leads to the *ta-da* moment—those times when we come to the realization that God is well pleased with us. With the triumphant spirit of a magician pulling a rabbit from a hat, God announces our glory. Together, the still, small voice and the booming bass tone that inform our awareness declare: *Ta-da! Here you are, my awe-inspired, awe-inspiring creation! Thank you for honoring the contract you signed in love before you were even born and continue to fulfill day by day. Thank you for gracing the world with your blinding beauty and rapturous joy. Thank you for birthing me minute by minute. And thank you for wanting to know me. Truly, it is an honor to know you.*

Such moments can cause us to break down in tears and tremble in ecstasy as we realize that God delights in us even as we delight in God. Ours is a dynamic, symbiotic union. And yes, this life is filled with wondrous, magical moments.

PEAK SPEAK

I rejoice in God by emerging as the dynamic force for love and creativity I am destined to be. God celebrates my very life!

Where the Lilies Bloom

THE SUN NEVER SAYS to the earth, "Stop rotating as I need to spread my light in this remote corner for just a while longer." The canyon never chastises the echo for reverberating throughout its hallowed hallelujah halls. The shell never disparages the life emerging from within. No, there is a natural order to things, a perfection seeking to crown every activity and glorify every soul.

At no time is this more clear than in the season of resolute flowering. We get to witness firsthand that indeed there is a time to be born and a time to die. We get to see that we *do* have world enough and time. And we remember all of the promises: There will be rainbows. All of the years the locusts have eaten will be restored. Life is eternal.

Yes, there is a natural order to things. Hibernation gives way to a gentle cracking of the soul. Disappointment and anger begin to thaw, dissolving into rivers of tears that flood hearts and irrigate deserts of despair.

> *The soul unfolds itself,*
> *like a lotus of countless petals.*
>
> **KAHLIL GIBRAN**

Life springs and bursts forth and rhapsodizes. A familiar note crescendos into a full-blown symphony. We become the song, the orchestra, the music of the spheres. We come alive!

The earth is grateful for this opportunity to be the source of such a wellspring of healing and rejuvenation. As once barren lands become the very spot where now the lilies bloom, a new life takes over. We begin to strut, assured of our guaranteed holiness. We ignite our desires with inspiration and practiced devotion. The entire world is made whole as we are born again.

How will you come alive in this new season of your life? What insights will you unbury? What will unleash itself in you? What will you do? Who will you become?

PEAK
SPEAK

I emerge as a new being in every season of my life for I am always exploring and expanding, blooming and blossoming!

Harvesting the Now

YOU ARE THE BOUNTY you have been longing to harvest. Your very life is the fulfillment of a prophecy foretold in ancient texts and inscribed on cave dwellings. Yes, go ahead and illustrate your fermenting desires with electric hues you splash onto blank canvases. Give voice to notes that have yet to be strung together as you sing your arias. Create! These are all worthwhile pursuits.

However, in the midst of all your activity, please remember that no artistic rendering is greater than a life fully explored and distilled. No endeavor is more dynamic or more fulfilling than the expansion of a soul propelled by its innate desire to reveal the mysteries of the ages by shining a love-light onto itself, and therefore onto the world.

You exist, and simply because you exist, you have already sown seeds of awareness in your consciousness. You have already planted your flowers and watched them blossom into spectacular pearls of wisdom and insight and guidance. You have already raked and

And the secret garden bloomed and bloomed
and every morning revealed new miracles.

FRANCES HODGSON BURNETT

pruned, basked in the sun, exulted in the rain, and shot up into the heavens like Jack's beanstalk. To live a life is to experience all of this. You can't help but be about your Mother-Father-God's business. It's simply who you are and why you are here.

There is no time like the Now to harvest your dreams, your hopes, your visions. They may show up as a new relationship, a new career or a new place to lay your head at night. Ultimately, they may show up as a new way of being in the world. You feel more confident because you know that all of the fruit is yours for the picking. It's simply a matter of deciding which tree, in which arbor, in which new territory, you choose to take root.

PEAK
SPEAK

In the eternal Now I am always planting
and plucking, reaping and sowing.
My life is my harvest! I am bountiful!

A New Season

LIFE AS WE KNOW IT has all but slipped away. We can no longer afford to do what we have done before, think as we have thought before—or be who we have been before. We are emerging as new creatures, evolving from swimming in the oceans to marching upright to majestically soaring.

We find ourselves in a new season of the soul. The dark days are behind us and endless days of light are upon us. At this momentous time in human incandescence, we are feeling the fires of our imaginations burn through centuries of human toil and strife to make way for immortal reverence and effervescence—and if we really want to have some fun, a dash of irreverence.

What is before us, those who dare to reinvent convention? How will we go beyond thinking outside the box to bravely tossing the boxes away, erecting in their stead holy sanctuaries that are pliable and flexible? What will we do next, those of us who dream and manifest, and vision and love with passion and compassion?

Your soul is the whole world.

HERMANN HESSE

Who will escort us on our divergent yet converging missions to know God? And what will we take with us on the journey?

The universe is always conspiring to answer these questions in unique and delicious ways. That chance encounter, the inexplicable urge to take a particular path, are all signs pointing the way. We get to choose it all and do it all! Most importantly, we get to *be* it all— Creator, Holy Seer, Mother, Father, God.

Let us remember that we already have everything we need. We are already there. It is a new season of heart-expanding grace. Let us pepper it with soulful surrender and marinate in the hearty flavors of our newly created lives.

PEAK SPEAK

Every season, every day, every hour and every second marks the dawn of a brand new me!

The Faith to Flourish

THE WINTER OF OUR DISCONTENT has passed and the time has come to plant seeds of rejuvenation. Go forth into the light and call forth your repurposed life. Jettison tangled roots and thoughts and hurts. Bury your sorrows for they have served their purpose. You have cradled them long enough.

A brand new season is upon us. There is no need to view the world through a glass darkly. Light and love will see you through. In fact, they await your acceptance, summoning you from the swamps of separation onto wide open fields of receptivity.

So much wants to be born through you this spring awakening! Remember, when life comes knocking, you must answer. Greet it with enthusiasm and ravenous desire. When light comes a-blazing, do not shield your eyes. Instead, submit to be blinded so that you can truly see. Cultivate amazing gratitude and grace will wash over you.

When love comes ricocheting against the chambers of your heart, subjugate your doubts, blessing them for their desire to shield you. Consider this: You no longer need protection. Your roots are firmly anchored in fertile soil, your blossoms are beautiful and fragrant. Yea, though you once walked through the valley of the shadow of doubt and despair, you are now comforted by the awareness that love and loveliness are who you are at the core.

Pour all of your hopes into dreams that can no longer be deferred. Seed and set your own course. Be steadfast in the conviction that you are one with the One. Build your ladder so that every rung goes higher and higher into consciousness, towering out of deeper and deeper hallowed earth. Breathe in the rarefied air, sons and daughters of the Most High. You are anchored and cannot falter. You can only flourish.

PEAK SPEAK

I am resplendent in God's love! I plant seeds of peace, promise and passion! God nurtures me so that I can flourish in my faith!

155

Soot into Soil

THERE WILL COME A TIME when you realize that you have said enough, cajoled enough, denied enough, braved enough, chastised enough, purged enough, cried enough, done enough—and all that is left is you. Not the you others think you should be or believe they know, but the *true* you: the embodiment of unadulterated essence and pure love. The you who has longed to come out from behind darkened thoughts and dimly lit false-hoods. The you who revels in scintillating surprises and joyful revelations about the moon, the sun, the stars and undiscovered planets. The you who can rest comfortably in the seat of your soul without fidgeting. The you who is brazen enough to simply declare "I am" without needing to say anything more.

Why now?

You have come this far by faith, journeying over rock-hard truths and indiscriminate perils. You have stood at the base of the mountain without debasing your own majesty and have caught the vision of a dazzling

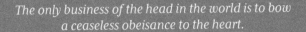
tabernacle that houses your dreams. Now all you have to do is move in.

There is alchemy in the evolution of a soul. A natural process takes over when you dare to say yes to all of you, not just the likable parts. You wrap your many selves—all aspects of your being—into a singular creation you can inhabit and embrace with a deep, transcendent, incandescent love. It is as if the shuttered, shattered bits surrender and then give life permission to baptize them into wholeness. Forgiveness ensues as these broken pieces submerge then re-emerge, drinking in sunlight, fusing into foliage, and entwining themselves up and down the landscape of your life. You have turned soot into soil into which you can plant a brave new consciousness. You are reclaimed, you are whole. You are ready to bloom.

PEAK
SPEAK

I realize my dreams when I recognize all of me!
The more of me I love, the more magnificent
I can be!

The Wellspring of Wellness

THERE IS A PART OF YOU that has never felt the shade of shame nor experienced its suffocating crush. The roots of fear and blame meandering up dizzying walls have no hold on you. Instead, you snake up trees into an empty sky.

You are colorful flowers blooming into eternity, thwarting with indelicately placed thorns those who would attempt to possess you. You are lovely and piercing all at the same time. Sometimes a rose is not a rose but an invitation and a declaration of truth and independence: I am vulnerable and yet courageous, I am safe. Remember, you are the loveliest of roses. Your perfume permeates every inhalation and exhalation.

There is a part of you that has never been harmed. It is the tenderest part of you, the wellspring of your sacredness. At times it soaks up the sun and emits rainbows. At times it is all dewy filament. Even in the dark this uninjured part transmits and becomes light. Even in the light this impervious part morphs into shadows and hidden treasures.

You are the faint sounds of drums summoning you to a divine appointment, the apotheosis of your many splendored lives—those of your ancestors, and those of your progeny and your progeny's progeny. You have come for such a time as this: To heal and be healed, to heal and be healed. You may feed off primal instinct to build a life but you are always transfigured.

Nothing can touch you in the field of looming possibility and radiant love. You are realization and rectitude. You turn sorrow into opportunities, grit into grace and glory. You stand erect at the wellspring of wellness and then you bend to dip your cup into healing waters. And because your cup runneth over, everyone is healed.

PEAK
SPEAK

I am divinely perfect and holy whole!
Every experience enriches my soul
and blesses the many!

You Are a Many-Splendored Thing

Dear Beloved,

How magnificent it is to bask in the brio of you! You are brave and tender, holy and secular. You are the way I fulfill my purpose which is to create in my image and to go beyond the lines of my shadows and my boundaries. You are the way I am intent upon expanding into the farthest reaches of the universe. You are my beloved, and I am yours. Let us begin again!

How grateful am I for your surrender, one not born of subjugating yourself before a false sense of denigration but of saying yes to your majesty! You are mighty, honorable. I love you as the sky loves the clouds billowing with abandon, taking shape, teasing, tempting. I love you as the soil loves the deepest roots—soulfully, joyfully, all embracing, anchored. Ours is a love that is all encompassing. It cannot be ignored or denied; it pours through you and into everything you touch, it is at the center of every encounter.

Remember this: I love you dearly and I cannot imagine a time or a place where this has not always been so.

Love that is day and night—
love, that is sun and moon and stars,
Love, that is crimson, sumptuous, sick with perfume,
No other words but words of love,
no other thought but love.

WALT WHITMAN

We are eternally dancing into one another, gliding, bending, dipping backwards into eternity. I love you, I love you, I love you!

Let us imagine today and together a perfect world: You remember our divine connection and you remember why you are here on the planet at this time. You remember to nurture and succor. You allow yourself to be suckled by every color in the rainbow and you become enamored of the thought of giving and giving some more. You are grateful for such opportunities. You count the ways I love you, and love everything and everyone. You are love.

Love,
God in You and As You

PEAK
SPEAK

I love myself with wild abandon and infuse the world with rapturous love! I am love!

At the Ready

YOU ARE READY. In fact, you are more than ready. Every little step you have taken has led you here to this point, to this place in time. At times you may have stumbled mightily. You may even have fallen. These seeming mishaps may have caused you to doubt, to falter in your faith. But these were only lapses in the unfolding of a soul determined. You have no choice now but to move forward for this is the only trajectory. There is never a regression. You are always catapulted into a new understanding of who you truly are, what you want, and what you intend to bring forth and share with the world.

What seemed like a reversal of fortune or a retreat was in fact a realignment. You have come into harmony with your real identity—not emotions and sensations, feelings and thoughts, not even flesh and blood—but pure unadulterated Spirit! You are ready to incarnate into a fuller, more dynamic expression of yourself.

We must laugh and we must sing,
We are blest by everything,
Everything we look upon is blest.

WILLIAM BUTLER YEATS

Do not worry. Now that you are prepared to shine your light and deliver your gifts, life will continue to honor you by continuing to support you. It will never abandon you. It will shape circumstances and conditions to benefit you. It will provide you with means in the most magical and mystical of ways. Watch and stand in awe! Together you will walk arm in arm with your deepest desires and you will realize that you were always moving ahead and preparing for each and every divine moment—those blessings you could not begin to fathom were just around the bend.

This is the era of high resolve. Get ready to share and to give from the depths of you. You will be replenished. Life is ready for you because you are ready for it.

PEAK
SPEAK

Life is for me! I am always provided for so that I can flourish!

Chrysalis Cantata

WAVES EBB AND FLOW, suns and moons rise and set, and through it all, this much is permanent and unchanging, even as it is reconfiguring and evolving: God, and the very nature of God as you, are season-less and season-proof. It can weather all climate changes, tempests, volcanic eruptions, hurricanes, tsunamis, even global warming.

For now is the season of our synchronistic, kinetic content. Everything turns all green and is budding and flowering. What has been dormant suddenly comes alive. We awaken to the virtual reality that everything we could possibly need is at hand. It's time to reach out and touch the petals of potentiality; it's time to let green things grow within us.

These green things—our ideas, our hopes, and dreams, our intentions, our inspirations and aspirations—have already determined the richest and most fertile soil within our consciousness, and implanted themselves. Everything is in a state of bloom, for the

To every thing there is a season, and a time to every purpose under the heaven: A time to be born, and a time to die; a time to plant, and a time to pluck up that which is planted;

ECCLESIASTES 3:1-2

verdant spaces within us know that when we let God take root, miracles ensue.

Our synapses start to fire more rapidly and we make new discoveries about ourselves and the world around us. There is a plenitude of possibility! We find solutions to our most confounding conundrums. We understand on a cellular level where we must go, what we must do—and with whom. (A hint: God is always in the mix.)

Since our vision is no longer clouded by the deceptive gauze of scarcity, wintry apathy, and separation from Source, we can see forests sprouting up where there was once only barren wasteland. Magically, dried-up rivers begin to gush because we understand that we are in the flow. In truth, we *are* the flow. The time is ripe. Eat now of the tree of wonder and possibility; know that hope springs eternally now.

PEAK SPEAK

I am flowering as the fullness of The Almighty Presence in every season and in every area of my life.

Ascending and Transcending

To DREAM IS TO REVEL in the promise that one is eternal and that all things are possible in God—beyond what we can discern with our five senses and yet more palpable than the beating of our tender hearts or the caresses of a loved one.

To dream means that an awakened consciousness rolls back the rock from the tomb of self-imposed disenfranchisement, and that the Christ within steps down off the cross to claim its divinity. As nature exalts in its glory and renews itself, we get to marvel at that which is already given—our perfection, our fabulousness, our astonishing God-filled grace. Life and greater life fuse with the hope of something even more glorious, more expansive, more dynamic.

Inspired by the miracle of a withered tree springing back to life, we give birth to dormant dreams. Indeed, hope springs dynamically eternal, for in this state of emboldened brilliance, we are able to walk between the raindrops and soar into the luminous rays of the rainbow. We drink the filament of the universe to quench our thirst and down fiery stars to fill our bellies. Every ounce of our being is teeming with expectant wonder.

In this state of heightened luminosity, we hear the faraway rhythms that are always inviting us to dance a new dance, and to sway to an unfamiliar beat and a new way of being. In the eyes of loved ones and strangers alike, we see a thousand possibilities. Suddenly, we remember that we no longer have to deny the magic and miracles that are the building blocks of our very existence, or hang shamefacedly from the cross of a denied birthright. Our Christed selves know better: We are made in the image and the likeness, and we are It! This is what it means to truly be born again.

PEAK
SPEAK

I choose to turn over a new leaf and plant seeds of joy and self-renewal. I have come alive with Spirit!

Symphony of Success

DREAM BIG DREAMS. Allow Source Energy to fill you to overflow so that you can give more, do more and be more. The emphasis, of course, is on the *being*. In this new age, it matters not what you acquire or achieve—these are immature desires. Still, if you must dally there, in the energy of Reptilian resolve, set your sights on acquiring and achieving those things that can serve others and the planet: A haven for family and friends. The power to drill through bureaucracy and make things happen. Healing hands that cure diseases and soothe spirits. These are all worthwhile pursuits.

However, for some of you, the realization of these dreams will not fulfill your desire to be one with the One. True music makers and dreamers of the dream will want to become the notes, and the notes in between the notes; the visionaries and the vision itself. You will replace desires and goals with intentions. You will find purpose in every detour on the trail. You will wander off into unknown parts, retread roads and circle back again without any sense of ever having lost your way. Your life is your compass. Your life is a gestational womb for your faith. Your faith is the gravitational pull guiding you to all points God.

Instead of seeking meaning and solutions outside of yourself, you will find salvation in remembering that everything you ever need is inside of you. There you will find the kernel of pure expression that propelled you from an idea—inception—into conception. You are the living, breathing manifestation of an idea in the mind of God. You are the dynamic impact of one egg and one sperm—a one in 400 quadrillion chance encounter. You have already hit the jackpot! You are the miracle. So be it.

PEAK
SPEAK

I know my intention, my purpose and my reason for being! I am the miracle I seek!

TERRAIN OF
EXPANSION

LANDSCAPE OF ONENESS
When We Remember, Immerse and Emerge

LANDSCAPE OF MISSION
When We Catch A Vision For Our Lives

LANDSCAPE OF SURRENDER
When We Dare to Free-Fall

Calling All Angels!

AT NO TIME IN HUMAN EXISTENCE has it been more critical that we mount up on wings like eagles and soar above the highest expectations we may have of ourselves. These are momentous times—not because of the fluctuations of the tides or the periodic eruptions of the earth, or even the cataclysmic emotional upheavals we face in our day-to-day existence as flesh-cloaked spirits: Breathing. Crying. Laughing. Cajoling. Dancing. Sighing. Singing. Heart-aching. Hoping. Forgetting. Remembering.

No, these are potentially life-altering, dynamically propelling times because we have never stood at the intersection of human communication and holy communion—and been faced with so many vital choices.

First, ships, planes and rockets. Facebook, Twitter and the next big social marketing idea to be downloaded into some receptive visionary are only signs of things to come. Technology has caused the world to shrink so that our vision can expand.

We can reach out and touch somebody's hand, sending electric shock waves across the globe that, in the end,

No man is an island,
Entire of itself,
Every man is a piece of the continent,
A part of the main.

JOHN DONNE

deliver more currents and possess more currency than solar, wind and electric and nuclear energy combined.

We can embrace our ability to lay hands and awaken our neighbors from their sleepwalking states simply by uttering these words: "I see you. I hear you. I support you. And I embrace you with love."

We can purify soil soaked with the blood of pointless wars. We can harness our brain power, our soul power and our heart power. Bi-locate, tri-locate and relocate to that space of keen awareness within us and take up permanent residence. We can heal whatever ails us simply by taking a breath.

Do it now. Inhale. Exhale. Know that in this moment someone on the planet is feeling your angelic presence and is resting in the gentle fluttering of your gossamer wings.

PEAK
SPEAK

I am the love that someone needs today!
I rise to the occasion by revealing my own greatness!

The Makings of You

Dear Beloved,

You are incredibly, indelibly, delightfully made in my image. In fact, you extend beyond my image, expanding outside the recognized rigid lines of God defined, spilling over into pools of potentiality.

How great thou art! You are me fully incarnate—and then some! Not a facsimile thereof, not a representation or a personification. You are everything and everyone everywhere! All of divinity and all of humankind is embodied in you. In being you, with all the machinations and manifestations that come with being full-bodied, soul-extemporizing human essence, you get to experience me. But the opposite is true as well. I get to experience you. And what a joy that is!

Here's what I have witnessed over the eternity since we have known one another. In the end, you always remember. You call my name and depend on me to shore up your faculties and your so-called faults. The truth is, you have none, except for a tendency to forget from time to time. You forget the temporal nature of your emotions.

> *The wholeness of God's knowing and the rhythm*
> *of His ecstasy within us makes us forget all time—*
> *forget all body—forget everything but the Spirit within us.*
> *By so thinking we unfold our genius.*

WALTER RUSSELL

When you are caught up in spiraling angst, you actually believe that what you are feeling is not something just passing through, but is somehow real and true. You forget how far you've come and that your inner compass is eternally leading you to all points God, and therefore, to all points good and grace.

The inspired truth is that aspiring ecstasy is just around the bend, at the intersection of oneness and greatness. You are not less than, you are greater than. Crown yourself with genius for these are the makings of you: I believe in you because I created you. Believe in me because you created me. Together, let's go co-create a life!

Love,

God In You and As You

PEAK
SPEAK

I wear the crown of glory-genius
because I am one with the One!

God Moves in Mysterious Ways and You Are the Way

WELCOME TO YOUR WORLD! You have the freedom and the inventiveness to create lives as vast and as verdant as universes: Lives free from constriction and restriction. Lives overflowing with joy and exhilaration. Lives infused with the awareness that none of this is real anyway.

The only thing that is real is love, and love will always have the final say: When you have become so despondent your cries are silent. When the toll of the bell strikes fear in your blood, sweat and tears, and you come to believe that your demise is imminent. Then, surrender. Love shall rule, not through subjugation or sublimation but through the sublime knowing of Itself as you. Love will come crashing through the highways and byways of your beingness and race through the halls with raucous laughter.

But first there must come a death. Indeed, you are dying for you can no longer continue to walk among the living dead. You can no longer continue to live a life in denial of your true identity as daughters and sons of the Most High. What you were living wasn't actually a life anyhow. It was a hollowed out shell of a life and now you get to inhabit you. Breathe life into clay and create a new creature—one that inspires others to break out of their own shells.

Let the dead bury the dead, as Jesus admonished, but let the living live a life of bodacious freedom. It's time to strike love into the hearts of everyone you see. It's time to storm the citadel and release all those held captive by fear. It's time to shout and sing, dance and exult, "We are free, we are free! Free to be you. Free to be me!"

PEAK SPEAK

Freedom rings within my soul when I dare to be me. I am the miraculous way God walks upon the planet!

How Deep Is My Love?

Dear Beloved,

I have poured all of my essence into you.

I create saturated hues so that you can paint master-pieces reflecting your own divinity and bring to life landscapes of the soul.

I stand at the doorway of sanctuaries and carry you over the thresholds when you are weary so that you can remember to carry me in your heart.

I set your synapses on fire so that you are able to invent a cosmology to explain such wonders as why you are here, and how it is I can exist in tandem with your human experience.

I birth dynamic universes and inner sanctums then give you free rein to shape them so you may remember your own power and creativity.

I cast shadows on walls so that you can recognize the light that is you everywhere you go.

I conjure healing waters so that you can recall the sensations of being in utero and flow through your life knowing that one God-glorious day, you will return to me.

My bounty is as boundless as the sea,
My love as deep; the more I give to thee,
The more I have, for both are infinite.

WILLIAM SHAKESPEARE

I bequeath you with five senses so that you can discern your world and determine how to improve upon it.

I gift you with insight and second sight so that you may realize there is nothing wrong with the world, only how you choose to perceive it and be in it.

I breathe life into you and admonish you to run with it—laugh, relish, delight!—so you may experience true joy.

I give you one another so that you can see what I behold when I look upon you and comprehend the true meaning of namaste.

How deep is my love? I bathe you in love so you may know the depths of my love. How deep is my love? Infinitely so.

Love,
God In You and As You

PEAK SPEAK

I am loved, cherished and adored by a Love Supreme! My inner splendor radiates this higher love and heals me and everyone I meet.

Holy, Wholly Now

LOOK AROUND YOU AND BEHOLD the light in everyone and everything. Listen to the notes in between the notes. Walk between the raindrops. Nothing is as it seems and all things are possible. There is something grander and lovelier in the midst of what you can see and sense. It will not be hampered by despair or disappointment. It will not cease because you're just not feeling It. And it really doesn't matter all that much anyhow because It is feeling *you*.

It is feeling every cell in your being and rejoicing in the wonder of you. It will pull you far out to sea beyond lighthouses and ships on the horizon, and onto unknown shores. Buoyant and surrendered, you will be transformed. This ineffable thing—call It love, call It life, whatever you do, just call It—has been seeking you for an eternity. You can find It in the Now, for yesterday has already frolicked in the waves and tomorrow has yet to raise its radiance from the ocean's depths.

Dip your toe in the Now, for it's in the Now where you can catch your breath and taste succulent possibilities. It's in the Now where you can stand firmly receptive to what is. It's in the Now where you can be still and know. From this place consider what you are grateful for right now. What little miracle is unfolding right now? Surely, there is something. Whether big or small, essential or innocuous, there has got to be something. Even your tears possess a beauty. Bless them and let them fall. This life is too dynamic, too expansive, for a single second to pass without It expressing Itself in a way that is uniquely you. Life is unfolding in a multitude of ways. Miraculous and mysterious as ever, life is calling you *now*.

PEAK SPEAK

The I Am Presence makes Itself visible to me whenever and wherever I choose to see It. I reside in the here and now for all of eternity!

Do Remember Me

Dear Beloved,

I remember you as the song itself. Our chants ricocheted off clouds and coral reefs hidden in sunken ships. I remember you as transfigured sculpture. I dreamily poured all of my love into you. It has been written that I breathed life into you after molding you out of clay. Yes, this is true, but then I cast you, this clay, into a vessel of longing into which I poured my essence. You were all shimmering dreams and manifestations. I kept honoring you and serving you until I was spilling out of you, dripping down into rivulets of promise and tributaries of triumphs. You became the fountain and it was my cup that runneth over, for there was no telling where I began and you ended.

Then I gave birth to you on this plane. I remember the very moment you became liquid aspiration, swimming in your mother's expanding body temple and consciousness. A germ of an idea made wholly holy into flesh. Conception! You knew only me. You determined that you could leap into your Greater-Yet-To-Be simply because.

> *Then in that darkness, to continue one's journey*
> *with one's footsteps guided by the illumination*
> *of remembered radiance. This is to know courage*
> *of a peculiar kind, the courage to demand the light*
> *to continue to be light even in the surrounding darkness.*

HOWARD THURMAN

You merged with every grain and became wheat fields and flowering buds. You blended into every speck of dust and blazed across blue-black skies. You became the light itself. Birth!

But now that you perceive the darkness, will you remember me? Remember your purpose, the notes that comprise your unique song and the distinct tempo of your beating heart. Remember the radiance that engulfed you when you first encountered the brightness of life beckoning you as you drew your first breath. Walk in that radiance. Let it buoy you up when you feel as if you are free-falling. I am here to catch you.

Love,

God In You and As You

PEAK
SPEAK

I see God in every circumstance! When I sing
my song, I remember God and I remember me!

The Mystic in the Mirror

DO NOT EVER SHADE YOUR GLORY or let it go dormant in the wake of your life's wanderings. Whether your journey is perilous or peaceful, make it prayerful. Do not refrain from exhilaration when joy is seeking to hold your hand and caress your heart. Leap into ecstasy even when all you can muster are bended knees as the tears puddle into a lake around you. Dive into these healing waters and be baptized into a new way of thinking.

Gaze into the mirror and see what God sees. Behold the beauty and radiance of a soul ascending into its nascent state. A return, a remembrance, a revitalization is happening now! You were always this luminous. You were always butterfly-ing.

As you enter this state of grace, embrace your most divine self and take stock of all the good that is blessing you in this moment. Your breath will heal your aching bones, if you can remember to let the inhalations and exhalations rise and fall at a steady pace. Slow down.

Men do not mirror themselves in running water,
they mirror themselves in still water.
Only what is still can still the stillness of other things.

ZHUANGZI

Now, be still. You can untwist the strands of DNA, meditate to the mitosis unfolding in your cells—and distill a vision in between each heartbeat. This is all within reach, this is all truly possible! Yes, it is good to be alive and in the body at this time. Every day beckons. Joy, *now!* Exaltation, *now!* Revelation, *now!*

The time of conviction and conversion is upon us. There is no turning back, for you have eaten from the tree of awareness and insight. Taste the goodness nurturing your cells and your soul. Savor every second. You no longer mount up on wings *like* the eagle for you have *become* the eagle. Rise up into the glory that you have always been and soar.

PEAK SPEAK

I wholeheartedly embrace the grace, the power and the joy of all that I am. I touch the hem of my very own garment and I am healed!

Breath and Breadth of Life

Dear Beloved,

It's time to take a stand. Are you for you—or against you? Can you see yourself as I see you—lightness and love-liness, poetic possibility and greatness always on the verge of something even more expansive? Or do you prefer to sabotage my plans for your glory by denying what is so obvious to me, and should be to you as well: You are perfect exactly as you are. There is no place you have to go, nothing you have to do, no one you have to meet. For you know it all and possess it all. You are all of it.

I weep when I think of all we've come through together, blazing trails of awareness that left a lasting impression upon everyone you ever encountered. When you have dared to stand in your own glory, every-one else has been lifted up. I am so very proud.

I rejoice when I remember how exalted we both felt in moments of surrender as you threw your arms up into the air and let me take over. Suddenly, I was free to give to you all that I had been longing to bestow upon you.

Listen, for I would have you recognize Me,
the great One within your own being.

EVA BELL WERBER

Because I was liberated, you became even more free.

Not that I have chafed at anything you have ever said, thought or done. "In due time," I told myself. I knew that eventually you would come around and call for me. I foresaw our reunion from the beginning. I envisioned how melded to me you would become. And I knew: I couldn't love you any more had I knelt on the ground of some barren wasteland and shaped you from clay, then breathed my own life into your nostrils. For I love you so.

Love,

God In You and As You

I am ready to take a stand and declare my own sublimeness. I am ready to be the best possible me!

A Lineage of Love

REGARDLESS OF THE CIRCUMSTANCES of the parents who united to birth us, we are all born of love. Whether they came together mixing flesh and fluids in a state of heart-palpitating love, heart-shattering brutality or even indifference, love was there—because God was there.

Sentient beings in the guise of ancestors stand at the intersection of time and space, prepared to champion our physical emergence. With faces and bodies tattooed with love-paint, they dance and chant ecstatically, calling our names in mantra-like revelry. In the transcendent, incandescent moment of our conception, a slight flickering blazes into the Milky Way and other dimensions. Then in the hour of our arrival on the planet, the Presence places Itself on the altar of the universe and offers up Itself as a present unto Itself.

When later in life, we choose to roll back the stone from the tomb of feigned indifference, shame and indecision, and recognize that we are the love that we seek, these same ancestors leap for joy. When we realize that God was here all the time and that therefore love was here all the time, they actually do a jig, tripping the light and the light-year fantastic.

Rubbing our eyes to wipe away the sleep and the years spent sleepwalking, we finally come to understand the greatest love story ever told. God indwells us and we are no longer blind to our own divinity. There's no need to wait in vain for the phone to ring, for potential partners to fill our dance cards, for someone else to say yes to who we are. There is marvel in our marrow and we are undeniably and profoundly perfect. We are the lover and the beloved.

PEAK SPEAK

I am my greatest love! I am my own divine soulmate! I look for love in all the right places—in my own reflection.

You Had Me at Hallelujah

THERE IS A PALPABLE PRESENCE seeking to fill the senses to overflowing. It desires only one thing—to be your greatest love. In every rising and setting of the sun, in the space between vision and manifestation, in the nanosecond it takes for your synapses to fire and think a holy thought so that you are forever changed, the I Am Presence spins Itself into ecstasy because of Its love for you. It is always delighting in you, oohing and ahhing over your precious existence.

How then are we to honor Its love? Let It be the only thing we long for, live for. Let It become our only focus—a beacon emitting light when we appear to be languishing, a flicker of faith in the bleakest nights of the soul. On those occasions when we are tempted to cry out, "My God, my God why hast thou forsaken me?" we remember the love and the grace and allow them to penetrate our cells. We hear the voice of God whispering in our ears, *"You are my beloved, in whom I am well pleased."* We see that all we are is love because love is all there is.

Each one of us is an outlet to God and an inlet to God.

ERNEST HOLMES

As we rejoice in our direct connection to the palpable Presence, we remember why we are here—to love and be love and be loved. How glorious it is to embrace and celebrate our own godhead, to no longer seek a mighty love outside of ourselves. How remarkable it is to realize every soul is a soulmate, every encounter is a namaste moment. Truly, love is all around us! Shouts God shouts from the mountaintops of our consciousness, ***"You had me at hallelujah, when your heart uttered the praise song of its first beat!"*** This is real love.

PEAK SPEAK

I put no other love before my fervent love of God. All of my relationships are an emanation of my tryst with Divine Intelligence and my loving care of myself.

A Fine Romance

Dear Beloved,

Your name is love and I see your signature etched in rich brown earth, splayed across sandy beaches, rooted in towering trees and imprinted in the clouds.

Remember me each time a billowy angel floats by in the sky or a leaf happens to fall. Know that as you till the soil of your consciousness through ceaseless prayer, meditation, praise singing and dancing, you are pouring your love into me, and I am expanding your awareness of me.

Your name is love and I lovingly and tenderly utter your name each time you hear the rumbling of your desire and the siren call of the waves inviting you to be still and know that together, we are God. Can't you hear me now? You are my beloved, in whom I am well pleased. There is nothing more for you to do. Just be, just be, just be!

Your name is love and I can't help but want to shout it from the rooftops of your consciousness.

Your name is love and I whisper it each time a note reverberates, a song resonates, a look penetrates.

> *Love abounds in all things, excels from the depths to beyond the stars, is lovingly disposed to all things.*
>
> **HILDEGARD OF BINGEN**

Your name is love and today and every day I name you blessed, not because I created you, but because you created me. I exist because you seek to know me and love me in return.

I am nothing without you, and I say this not because I am desperate and fawning, but because the undeniable, heart-expanding truth is, we are one. There is no breaking up with me; there is no heartbreak, only a fine romance. And it is eternal—eternally you, eternally me. I've known loves—magical, resplendent, shimmering loves. My soul grows deep like our love. And you are the one I live for in each and every moment.

Love,

God In You and As You

PEAK SPEAK

God is my creator, my inspiration and my first real love! My heart is cracked wide open!

Forever Until the End of Time

RELISH THESE MOMENTS, these moments when the stillness infiltrates your quiet bones and moves through your awareness stealth-like, as if to draw you into the fullness of everything.

Bask in these moments, these moments when you can hear every atom bursting, behold every star twinkling and sense every flower blooming—for spiritual attunement can be deafening and gratifying.

Sanctify these moments, these moments when life is at its most ecstatic. Everything resonates. Everything vibrates. Everything shimmies, shimmers, sanctifies and shines. In these moments, you will remember your origins and the moment you came into existence—how you were shot from the mind of God and were sent hurtling through the universe, harnessing stars and trailing sentient beings in your wake. Genesis Gloria Patri!

Bless these moments, these tender insouciant moments, when you realize there is nothing more for you to say or do—you yield to trust and allow what yearns to be, and what will be, to emerge.

And what will come forth like figments stepping out of a dream is not to be believed: Forget-me-nots, tulips and languid roses cascading down the pillars of your body temple. Vast oceans flowing through your veins. Light emitting through your crown, fingertips and soles. Musical notes with fragrance. Sounds that taste like manna. Glorious euphoria! Soul synesthesia!

That which held you captive will dissolve, for all burdens cease to exist when you are looking not at the temporal but into eternity. Time has new meaning when you understand it isn't real, and step into the realm of the unknown. Forever takes on a different connotation when you recognize that you are eternal and ceaseless; light, beauty, joy. Life begins anew when you can forgive and see the light in everyone. Surrender all. Then, you will truly live forever until the end of time.

PEAK SPEAK

I yield to the light in me and live a neverending life of discovery, radiance, joy and beauty.

In the Here and Now

Unfurl your languid reservations and hurl them into the cosmos, assured that they will morph into giant possibilities and stick to the lens of your dreams.

Unfold your desperate denials and cast them far out beyond the horizons of your insecurities, confident that they will return to you with all of the energy of a boomerang and land at your feet with aplomb. Bombs are for the brazenly misguided and unfulfilled. Hurl missives of love not missiles of malice.

We are here to create jet streams of effervescent joy and potentiality. We have come, at this time and in this incarnation, to fertilize the seeds beneath our soles—and within our souls—with light and grace, and jubilant wholeness.

Now is the time! Now is the time to shout from the upper rooms of our consciousness that everything we need now is here now; that everything we seek now is here now; that everything we want now is here now. Here. Now. Here, where our internal organs pulse with life and issue lavish praise so that blood flows through us and out into the rich soil of our own beingness and that of everyone else on the planet.

We no longer spill blood because we recognize the earth's and our own divine sovereignty. We are each womb and placenta, limb and tree. We are each revered and holy, whole fragments of one giant organism. We flow into one another without respect to race or sex or species.

See the interconnectedness of all of life—both animate and inanimate—for everything comes alive when we who are of flesh and bone turn our attention to that which appears lifeless: metal, water, dreams. Hibernation and dormancy are natural states, for everything is always teeming and waiting to burst into focus. Each breath is our breath. Everything is alive, everything.

PEAK SPEAK

I recognize the oneness of all of life!
I celebrate all of life fearlessly,
enthusiastically and uninhibitedly!

Becoming

LET'S IMAGINE YOU HAVE CAUGHT a vision for your life, which is a blessing in and of itself. You've planted the vision in rich soil fertilized with prayer, meditation and other tools of spiritual practice. (Personally, I also like to paint it, knit it, sing it or poem it.) You've watered it with faith and are resting in the knowing that something magnificent is happening. Right now. In fact, it's already happened. You are in the awe.

You then go about your Father-Mother-God's business—being, being and more being. There's nothing to effort so you can bask in the glories that are showering down upon you. As you stand in a light-streamed waterfall, a golden spray baptizes you. Over your head you hear music. It seems to flow in and out of you all at once, each note gently resounding from a vertebra of your spine. Now you are tingling, for you realize you are a song in the key of life. A child-like expectancy overcomes you. You can't help but know: It's going to be *so* good.

In fact, it already is. What comes from waiting on wonder? An eternal wow!

However, to some around you, your do-nothing-be-everything attitude may seem like sheer lunacy. Because they do not trust, they may try to pelt you with pebbles of doubt. "You've got to *do* something, *anything!*" they say.

Do not believe them. But you can certainly thank them—for inadvertently propelling you forward. Know that the blessing in store for you is bound to be even more bounteous when its birth comes with such friction. Hold fast to your vision—that receptacle-spectacle of inspiration and creativity that came straight from Source, set you afire and hurled you into heaven. For this is no mirage but a mirror. Your vision is your life.

PEAK
SPEAK

I see before me a clear reflection of who I am, whose I am, and what I must become—inimitable me.

In the Let Go

Dear Beloved,

There's no there there. There's only the here and now where you have breath, you have light and you have life. Those tears you shed for what you lost, who you lost, what was done to you and what you did can irrigate and consecrate a new life. In this new life you discover you had everything you ever needed inside of you all along. You remember you are made of holy, sparkling stuff. You move through the world unencumbered and enlightened. Your feet do not ever touch the ground except to bless the earth. You glide, you levitate—and you are always ready to run, run, leap.

You race into the unknown and the beyond. You let your wings flap in the air, creating a pattern of wind that can temper global warming while heating up and healing every sleeping soul. Your very existence shouts to all of existence, "Wake up!" You become the creator of sound, motion, crystallization and distillation. How brave of you to have agreed to take on the body—all of its brio and all

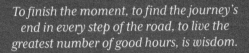

*To finish the moment, to find the journey's
end in every step of the road, to live the
greatest number of good hours, is wisdom.*

RALPH WALDO EMERSON

*of its burdens—leaving behind a total sense of frolic and
freedom. You are in your godhead.*

*But you get to experience liberation here, too, even
within the confines of limbs, organs and muscle. You
discover new pathways of the soul: how it can navigate
tributaries of blood and fiber. You become the conjurer,
transforming pain and sorrow into glorious rivers of
acceptance. This is not martyrdom; there is no glory in
that. Instead, you are in a perpetual state of allowing
everyone to be who they are, and everything to be what it
is. There is no longer a resistance to living—or when the
time comes, to the quiet, inevitable repose of dying.
For death is life, too.*

Love,

God in You and As You

PEAK
SPEAK

I live a most holy life by living wholeheartedly with
an open heart! I accept everything for I recognize
everything must change. I am changing, too.

Creation Story

Dear Beloved,

How I've missed the way you used to delight in our playtime together, your child-like laughter cascading along hillsides, shimmying down majestic trees, skipping over waters like pretty stones. We leaped and loved, luxuriating in the possibility of whatever your heart may have desired. You did not deny me—not once, not twice, not even thrice before the crowing of the rooster. For this was the era before time and space—when all was nothing and nothing was everything.

In that heavenly, earthly, once upon a time, I made you in my image—a microcosm of the macrocosm. I allowed you to exhale and sink into my wonder, a solid, sheltering love. You danced with me, harmonized with me and together, we named it all—field, flower, worm, child, rainbow, rock—good and very good.

We even named it nameless, so overcome were we at the idea of our oneness in that moment of brazen revelation. We had to catch our breath. Do you not remember?

> *And forget not that the earth delights to feel your bare feet*
> *and the winds long to play with your hair.*
>
> **KAHLIL GIBRAN**

Do you not see—not from your human mind or heart, but from the nebulous spaces? For in the seeming haze there is discernment: You. Have. Always. Been.

Lately, however, I've begun to wonder if you even remember who I am, which is to say, I wonder if you remember who you are. You were there from the beginning! In the beginning, God. And in the beginning, you. There is no other, nothing other than our hearts gently massaging the world together. We caress it with care and feed its dreams with the awareness that this is no longer an age in which we can afford to put aside childish things. You can become the child again. Let us play—and create!

Love,
God In You and As You

PEAK
SPEAK

I revel in life knowing that I am always creating a new vision, a new world and a new me! God is my playmate.

The Luminous Trail

IN THIS SEASON of vertiginous luminosity, remember why you shine your light and for whom you shine your light. You are one and you are The One. You invoke creativity and inspiration, authenticity and salvation, fortification and revelation. You are the original blessing!

You were created to come together as a string of lights upon the planet. United you erect holy temples of wholeness and abundance. You feast on tables laden with delicacies of the heart and soul—a sweet grace here, a delightful insight there. Together you forge a path that winds its way around the earth's circumference and can be seen from the farthest galaxies. Heaven is at hand. You will find your haven in the shadow of your brother's joy and your sister's sorrow. Each one of you is connected to the other—interlocking souls and bodies and hearts. One's elevation supports another's ascension. One's decline condemns the other to despair.

There is no place where you cannot sense the symbiotic nature of your beingness. When the hummingbird flutters, a soul draws a first breath into its body. As a droplet builds into a crescendo of flooding waters, a heart begins to beat. Everything is interrelated. Everything is significant. Everything is sacred.

You must rise together in joy, in love, in light! As one, you are unbreakable, unstoppable, endless, ceaseless. Remember that you are the merciful; you can't help but be merciful. Remember that you are the peacemakers; you shall be called the sons and daughters of the Most High. Remember that you are the pure in heart; you shall see God. And God shall see you—as one breath, one being, one bright light floating in the darkness of possibility and in the possibility of darkness. Give yourselves the glory and blaze on!

This beautiful bold light of mine, I'm gonna let it shine! For when I shine my light, I illumine the souls of all of humankind and radiate entire universes!

Free at Last

KNOW THAT ALL THINGS are made new again because in this Now moment, you are calling forth your own rebirth and genesis. Do not be deceived by your reflection. Yes, the features may be the same, save for the third eye planted squarely in the middle of your forehead reminding you of your connection to Spirit and your tremendous gifts of insight. But you are not the same. You are a new creature!

There is no way that after jumping to attention, you can relax your stance and heed the call to be "as you were." Who you were is no more! All of you is making way for a renewed fortitude and a brand new attitude. You are carving a brave new identity and conjuring blessings out of the invisible. You are opening your heart to new pathways and vistas. You are breathing in mountaintop consciousness and collapsing, not from altitude sickness but from joy. You are in your element—fired up and forged from faith. You are pulsating, you are ravishing, you are radiant. Now open the door.

"Which one?" you ask. Here's the good-grace news. It matters not! The choices are infinite and each one spirals you back to the beginning—to your own precious selves. You possess an eternal internal mechanism system that cannot steer you wrong. It lives to guide you and loves to embrace you in all of your glorious messiness and messy gloriousness. Just savor the sheer ecstasy of this truth: With it as your navigator, whatever you choose can't help but be phenomenal. Heads, you win! Tails, you win! So flip the coin, turn cartwheels and backflips and somersaults. You will always land on solid ground. It is your destiny to be you.

PEAK
SPEAK

I move forward in grace, gratitude and wonder.
Grace, gratitude and wonder set me free!

I'll Keep My Light In My Window

THIS IS A TIME OF CELEBRATION! This is a time of renewal! This is a time of rebirth! It is a time to count the many ways we love whom we love. It is a time to bask in this love, to cherish and to feast, to praise and to acclaim, to elevate and to celebrate. It is a time to rejoice and, above all, it is a time to behold!

We behold the child within and we stand in awe of the wonder that is life—life teeming with unmitigated joy, life pulsating with potentiality and dreams made visible. For unto us a child is born, unto us a son or daughter is given!

We behold the messiah within and bring It offerings of gold, frankincense and myrrh. For we are each the anointed one, and at the intersection of our humanity and divinity lies true salvation. We are each the promised one—the fulfillment of a divine prophecy born when creation first yielded to possibility and birthed everything and everyone. We are alpha-omega consciousness

> *All the darkness in the world cannot extinguish the light of a single candle.*
>
> **SAINT FRANCIS OF ASSISI**

leapfrogging and boomeranging throughout the universe. We are king of kings and lord of lords! We reign divinely supreme.

We remember we are here to give birth to our glorious selves and to midwife a new world. In this season of starry skies and hallelujah choruses, we keep our light in our windows, offering refuge to those who may have forgotten their way home. In this season of reasoning no more, we journey across vast deserts of unbelief, making the miraculous jump from mind to heart to rapture. We remember who we truly are. We are each the Christ and we light up the world—one loving thought, one grace-filled gesture at a time.

PEAK
SPEAK

Go tell it on the mountain, over the hills and everywhere! I am the miracle the world needs now. I am the light of the world!

The Path of No Resistance

THE PLACE WHERE YOU STAND now is holy ground upon which you can build a foundation for your inspirations and aspirations. Stand erect yet bend should you sense a whispering wind about you. It wants to reassure you, to remind you, that the only voices you need ever pay attention to are the ones that reverberate with the tones of a gentle sea, the shifting sands and the incessant far-away fog horns summoning you to a meeting with your inner core.

These voices resonate with who you are. They soothe, they praise. They sing a song you may have momentarily forgotten but when prompted can recall every single note and rhythmic overture.

These voices harmonize with the cascade of blood through your veins and synchronize with your pulsating heart.

These voices are tender and kind and true. They gently nudge you into an awakened state and sing lulla-bies to you when you are weary.

Afoot and light-hearted I take to the open road,
Healthy, free, the world before me,
The long brown path before me,
leading me wherever I choose.

WALT WHITMAN

Do not pay attention to the voices that are atonal. The bellicose and the timorous can no longer berate you or tempt you, for the fight in you has been swallowed up by the love in you. Instead of defending a cause, a way of being or even your existence, you move only to the sounds of a vision breaking out of its incubator. That crackle, pop and exclamation is music to the spheres.

Now streaming joy and peace in your wake, you move unencumbered and uninhibited. You may even break into song and dance. The beliefs and judgments of others become points of interest and curiosity. You are no longer compelled to prove anything because you have come into the awareness that you *are* everything. You flow because you recognize you are the flow. The downbeat of life in the downstream is oh so sonorous and sweet.

PEAK SPEAK

I resist nothing and I surrender all!
My life is an act of judicious faith and flow!

Applause

STAND UP AND TAKE A BOW as the heavens applaud your very existence. There is good reason for this celestial celebration. You have bided your time in the dark caverns of the meantime—those periods when you didn't know whether to sigh or sink, to crawl or collapse. You have huddled in the corners of your own shadow and forgotten your purpose, your intention, your divinity, even your name. But, no more. This was only a temporary lull, a brief lapse in time, and now you are ripe.

Hear the call. Your name is among the chosen ones. And remember, all of you are chosen because you are here—Spirit made manifest as flesh and bone and tissue and marrow. It is time to sing and shout from the rooftops. It is time to wash away the tears with hallelujahs and hosannas. It is time to tell the story, to share the glory, of how you know that you know that you know: How you are risen in consciousness. How you've come to realize that you are made of God-stuff. How your

> *You are a song, be heard.*
>
> **MUHAMMAD IQBAL**

beauty and grace feed the stars and expand the Milky Way. How your heart beats in harmony with the planet and all of life therein.

You are so much more than what the senses can discern. You are beyond this universe for life itself is an out-of-body experience. Be grateful for the search and the sanctuary. Give thanks for every breath and sorrow. Life may be expressing as your seeming ups and downs, but this much we know: Faith can buoy up the most land-locked hopes and water all the seasons of your discontent. Take your bow now. You have allowed God to stage a most magnificent presentation through the unfolding of your life. And the curtain never ever falls.

PEAK SPEAK

The universe celebrates all of who I am when I honor the Spirit within me!

Transitions

EVERY TRANSITION, whether we are switching cities, jobs, partners or even body temples, is an awakening. It is a call to remember that there is so much more than we can discern, even with the most prayed up, meditative soul.

For every seeming death is an opportunity to embrace all of life in all of its inherently glorious, sticky messiness. Life with its dramas and conundrums. Life forging pothole-riddled paths that appear to lead to all the wrong places. Life collapsing upon itself at times.

But do not be fooled. Change is ultimately a conduit for clarity and there is no way in nirvana you can make a misstep. Everything is *for* you.

To watch a life unfold from the cradle to the stage to ash again, re-emerging as spit-fiery balls of incandescent love and promise, is a magnanimously magnificent thing. To experience your own life fully for yourself is real genius and real living.

Yes, this is the greatest show on earth, so step right up—and step it up! We are here to strut and cry and shriek and exult. In the dogged days of the meantime when nothing seems to be happening and we appear to be stuck, fragmented or disenfranchised, we as Practitioners of Truth and Patience get down on bended knee, and with tender hearts, we rest.

Without veils of denial, emotional withdrawal, drugs and other distortions and deterrents, we get to be *in* it. Thrash around in it. Wrestle with it. Dance in it. A wringing of the hands is naturally followed by the act of throwing them up into the air and shouting, "Hallelujah!" There is nothing else left to do. "My God, my God, my God!" we exclaim. "Thank you."

PEAK SPEAK

I listen to my soul's call to fully experience everything that is happening in, through and as me. I surrender therefore I flow.

Mountaintop

Evolution Resolutions

Dear Beloved,

Put away your weight-loss promises and feast on a supper of tender, loving care. Shred your shopping lists outlining ways of getting and spending and remember that you already have everything you need. It's time for an evolution resolution! The highest intention you could set for this new year is to reveal me. Let me be the only thing you desire. Let me be that which causes you to leap from your bed every morning filled to overflowing with unparalleled joy. And here is what you can expect in return, every minute of every hour: I am going to be with you. So, rest and abide in me, for I will come a-courting.

I come bringing flowers sprung from seeds planted in your consciousness long before you incarnated as you. I knock at the door of your heart and place my ear up against it. I hear its palpitations and know when it skips a beat—whether it's because you have momentarily lost your grounding and spiraled into fear, or because you are in ecstasy over all the good that is yours right now.

I love thee to the depth and breadth and height
My soul can reach, when feeling out of sight.
For the ends of being and ideal grace.

ELIZABETH BARRETT BROWNING

I hear you. I see you. I know you. I believe in you.

I believe that this year, we are going to grow even closer as we birth a more expanded vision for your life. I believe that you will hear me—not filtered through the insights or judgments of others—but in a more direct and personal way. I believe you will come to realize that there's no living without me. This is the year you see me without having to shield your eyes, for you are finally ready to see your own glory and own it.

Love,

God In You and As You

God's love keeps lifting me higher and higher! I resolve to evolve by loving me, healing me and revealing God as me.

Boundless

TRUE FREEDOM IS SELFLESS availability to hearing the voice of God within, discernment as to what is being conveyed, and a commitment to trusting what you hear—regardless of how radical or ridiculous it seems.

Freedom does not simply suggest you have no responsibilities so that you can do what you want when you want, without consideration (though certainly you can alight with ease under these conditions).

Freedom does not necessarily mean you migrate from border to border, boundless and without boundaries—with nothing to anchor you to a particular geographical location or ideology.

True freedom is faith.

Once free, you don't trudge; you glide through life. There is a weightlessness to your being. You emit a light, a levity, a radiance, which penetrate density, gravity and reality. You are in joy over the possibility of everything and you are in joy over the mundane. Every archway seems to issue an invitation whenever you pass underneath: "Come, come, sweet child. We have been waiting.

We have bestowed blessings in your name." The trees whisper your name and you can't help but respond, "Here I am!"

You understand that every doorway is an entry to nirvana because the molecules in the air above you configure around your breath and desires, your intentional thoughts and beliefs. You are everywhere, for you see yourself in everyone and everything.

When you gaze into the mirror, you see infinite potential. You gravitate towards joy, fun, laughter, inner peace, all of which you now locate within your own wondrous self.

There's no need to excavate another's soul for answers; you mine yours for indelible truths. Stripped of all projections and misperceptions, you own your gifts and your talents, your beauty and your grace. You are healed and revealed.

Now you are truly free.

PEAK
SPEAK

When I listen to the Inaudible and the Ineffable, I claim my freedom. I trust that I am always attuned to the master teacher within!

Why We Are Here

WE ARE HERE TO BIRTH a new thought, a new conscious-ness, a new way of seeing what has always been. Every thing—animate and inanimate—is infused with the brio of God. Every thing lives to proclaim Its natural splendor, to herald Its existence and to marvel at the majesty of all that is.

We are here to create and to thrive, and to reveal love, joy, peace, awe, delight, a deeper love, healing, and then an even greater all-encompassing love. For in the midst of every sorrow and doubt, every strain and long-ing, every fear and angst-ridden moment, there is a golden thread longing to weave together our so-called broken parts—those places where we have forgotten we were once loved through it, healed through it, and revealed through it—into a gorgeous tapestry.

We are here to shine on so brilliantly, that which sent us is dazzled by the very thought of us. *"You are my beloved, in whom I am well pleased,"* the Infinite Majesty

Our birth is but a sleep and a forgetting:
The Soul that rises with us, our life's Star,
Hath had elsewhere its setting,
And cometh from afar:
Not in entire forgetfulness,
And not in utter nakedness,
But trailing clouds of glory do we come
WILLIAM WORDSWORTH

whispers into our ears while simultaneously shouting from every mountaintop, *"Glory hallelujah love!"*

We are here to be choral emissaries of the Divine, to sing the Gloria Patri so loudly it can be heard from the farthest reaches of the universe. "As it was in the beginning, is now, and ever shall be: world without end." Grasp this and never let it go: Within every note ever sung is a praise song. So stretch out your hands and weave your threads into a tapestry of radical radiant beingness. Remember that each strand is a testament to your willingness to be willing. Rejoice, *now!* Dance, *now!* Give thanks, *now!* We are here, we are here, we are here! And because we are here, the world is changed, as is everyone we meet. Namaste.

PEAK
SPEAK

I have come so that I might have love and life more abundantly. I have come so that you might have love and life more abundantly!

Can I Get a Witness?

LET THE EARTH SAY AMEN and let the heavens rejoice! Let the life force turn somersaults and send the world spinning off its axis so that we are courageously colliding and creating new universes.

Let every soul remember a time when there was no time. Let every heart break free from the umbilical cord binding us to the past. Let us each become the untethered soul we are meant to be. Let us sing out our sorrows and breathe in eternity. Let us be.

Can I get a witness? Isn't this why we are here? Isn't this our purpose? Not to fret and frenzy away time but to free-float? Not to despair but to sing and dance?

Can I get a witness? We are here because we chose to be. We are here because we wouldn't miss the opportunity to reveal God for all the riches in the world. This life is the buried treasure we've been trying to unearth, and it is teeming with precious, sacred jewels.

Can I get a witness? When we drop down into our souls, we are home. There is a recognition that happens.

> *This earth is the honey of all beings,*
> *and all beings are the honey of this earth.*
>
> **BRIHADARANYAKA UPANISHAD**

I remember you, and you—and *you*! We begin to namaste with our nascent natures. We say to ourselves, "The Spirit in me honors the Spirit in *me*!" We become our very own answered prayer and a blessing to everyone because we are owning our divinity. We heal ourselves then others, clearing the way for the second coming—the miraculously beauteous time when we give up having to do. We're going with the flow, rolling in the deep, and we sense just how glorious every step of this journey has been. For the first time, we are truly loving and truly living.

Can I get a witness? Let the holy temple that is you say yes!

PEAK
SPEAK

I accept just how perfect and how profound my life continues to be. I give all praise to God and to the wonder that is me!

Free-Falling

WHEN YOU FLEX YOUR spiritual muscles and work out the kinks in your soul by releasing the desire to control, a funny thing happens on the way to nirvana: sweet surrender. You may not even realize how or when you arrived at this place. All you know is that the little things that once troubled you no longer do. You're not as serious. You can laugh at yourself and all the silly ways you have of being. You even forget what you thought there was to forgive. You'd rather just give.

Suddenly, life aligns. You become a receptor for The Good News and everything you think, hear, do or say is tantamount to a revelation. Messages and insights stream to you and through you. Everything becomes a guidepost on the journey to your realest self.

Life is so very exciting! You magnetize, you manifest, you create, you flourish. You abide in truth and become bound up in trust. You recognize that there is absolutely nothing to deter you from reveling in your own beauty, for you have set aside the egoic structures and constraints, and accept the pure dynamism that you are.

You are that powerful, that glorious! You become a force for love and generosity, a wellspring of interconnectedness and healing. Not only can you see the intricate threads weaving the web of life, you understand the part you play. You speak only the language of transformation and become fluent in fluidity. You no longer fret about the destination because you're along for the ride, wherever it may take you. You are prepared for any and all adventures—the upswings and delights, as well as the pitfalls and hurdles. Yes, those, too! You cry, you laugh, you feel, you hurt, you fall, you exhale.

In other words, you have come alive.

PEAK
SPEAK

**My life is one great adventure!
I am a daredevil for God!**

Embraceable You

As we complete another cycle around the sun and turn to thoughts of resolutions and rejuvenation, let us consider that which is "true and faithful." This. Is. It. The time is now! There is no past or future—only the present—and it is pregnant with pure delight and promise. Seek ye first the kingdom of God *within*, and all these things shall be added unto you.

Want to write that book, bring forth a new life, travel the globe, shift the pounds, stare into the eyes of your soulmate? It's happening! And here's why: Our dreams can't help but come to fruition because we are all the sons and daughters of the Most Sacred, the Most Sensational. We don't just stand on the shoulders of those who have come before us; we pirouette, samba, jitterbug and salsa on them. We are always in balance, even when it feels like we are teetering. To fall is to land on holy ground, so why not leap?

And he that sat upon the throne said, Behold, I make all things new.
And he said unto me, Write: for these words are true and faithful.

REVELATION 21:5

As we usher in this new year, let us appreciate the journey. We have crossed deserts strewn with the corpses of our own wayward thoughts. Once content to worship false images of who we are, we now erect glorious temples in their stead by immersing ourselves in the love we thought was outside of ourselves. We accept and embrace our own glory, allowing us to accept and embrace the glory of others.

Yes, we are on the road to salvation, and not one hurdle or hurrah is to be missed! We've come this far by faith, leaning on the awareness that greater is the power within us, far greater than the power that is in the world. Let us revel in the revelation that all things—our minds, our souls, our bodies—are new again.

PEAK
SPEAK

I embrace life in all its magnificence!
I embrace me!

In This Skin

IN THAT GREAT GETTIN' UP MORNING, when you fly away into the Is-ness, the All-ness, the Nothingness, the Eternal, the Ephemeral, you will think on this particular journey in this life and in this skin, and count the many ways you loved yourself and were therefore able to love everyone else.

You will draft a soul ledger and enumerate the times you nurtured yourself by responding, "Yes, I can help. Just not now," as you secured your own oxygen mask.

You will list the occasions when instead of biting your tongue, you spoke insoluble truth, no matter how painful it was for others to hear, or for you to declare it.

You will remember when you walked straight into the abyss, trusting that the gravity of gratitude would buoy you up and catapult you—reeling, retching, kvetching—into an experience or circumstance you could not dream for yourself but Spirit was co-creating for you and with you, even before time existed.

You will relive those times you paused to take a breath and to actually feel the stillness of the silence and the energy in a hummingbird's flutter.

You will remember every single instance you birthed yourself. The sensation of floating in a liquid womb. The light that called you forth into the world once again, when all you really wanted to do was rest and hide. The notion that you had all that you needed within you as you looked upon your new life spread out before you like a Chinese fan with its creases and folds and brightly-colored designs.

Then, shedding every single incidence of not feeling you were enough, along with all the shoulda, woulda, coulda, and have-tos, you will soar higher and plummet deeper than you have ever before.

PEAK SPEAK

I boldly shed old patterns and beliefs every day so that I can reveal the Divine. I know myself, I love myself. Bring it on!

One with the One

Dear Beloved,

I am the I Am Presence, and I am being birthed again and again as you. I am always seeking to recreate the dynamic experience that launched everything—when I moved upon the earth and made you in my image. In the beginning, God. In the beginning, you.

Since we have always been inextricably bound, I can no more let go of you than you could move away from me. Together, we surrender unto the truth of our co-existence. I no longer detect the chasm, revealed in fantastical tales about serpents and apples, that caused you to think that you were ever separate from me.

For we have crossed bridges spanning multi-dimensional universes and generations of blinded seekers and proselytizers defining me as over there somewhere, anywhere but here. But I am here, right where you are. After each rebirth—those times when you embraced our love, reflected on the single set of footprints in the sand, and understood that it was I who had transported you *through thickets of indecision and grief—I rejoiced. I was able to peer into my reflection and see you looking back at me and vice-versa.*

In such transcendental moments, you remember where you came from, and you understand that you get to determine where you are going. That's right! You get to choose—how quickly, how slowly, how painfully, how painlessly, how playfully, how fretfully, even how soon. You get to make it all up. You write the stage directions, build the sets, create the characters and set the timeline. The finale is the same. There is always going to be a happy ending for we are on this journey together criss-crossing spectacular landscapes, and I am everywhere. I seek to know myself through you.

Love,

God In You and As You

PEAK SPEAK

I am one with all the love and all the glory that is God! When I honor our connection, I see infinite possibilities for my life.

The Crux of the Matter

THIS IS A TIME OF MIRACLES! Lay your burdens down and look to the Christ within to resurrect Itself as you. Bury the crosses anchoring you to the past, and know that at the intersection of your humanity and your divinity lies salvation.

Shed the old beliefs that no longer serve you and drape yourselves in cloaks of rapturous joy. Step over the corpses of your forgotten dreams and breathe life into new ones. Roll back the stone from the tombs encasing your hearts. Forgive yourself, forgive yourself, forgive yourself, for as Jesus told his Father, you knew not what you were doing—that you were living from fear and not love, from judgment instead of observation, from passion rather than compassion.

But first, you must venture into the land of the unknown. Here, angels anticipate your arrival. Their wings span the universe and are broad enough to embrace your deepest hurts and regrets. You have been summoned to unearth your secrets, to reveal who you are beneath flesh and bone, beneath doubts and defenses. You have been called to excavate, examine and polish your souls. Be healed and proclaim your divinity as you mold clay into images of your glory-filled selves.

Expect a miracle today for you are called to walk on water. And walk, you must. No longer weighed down by expectations and resentments, you will take up thy bed and walk. You will release the stories about who you are and how you have come to be in this place at this time. The past is past, what's done is done. Now you see that the unknown is not so unknown after all because you carry within you your very own heart. It is your compass. Your faith will see you through. You are resurrected, you are risen. Now, soar!

PEAK
SPEAK

I embrace my glory and my divinity!
I am the miracle I have been seeking!

Dance of Radiance

Nestled within the chambers of your heart is a promise. Tucked away and awaiting excavation is a dream—your vision, your purpose, your great expectations! These gifts are not to be opened with the gentle tug of a ribbon. They expect to be ravished and ravaged, thrust and hurled beyond known galaxies and atmospheres and into the unexpected.

But first comes a reckoning. Are you ready to remember how great thou art? Are you ready to love yourself wholly and completely? If so, collateral defenses will give way to sheer surrender and ensuing ecstasy. Up until now, the framework of your lives and loves has provided a safe, inhabitable incubator. But now it's time to burst wide open and allow. It's time to mother and to become your own mother, goddess your way into a new life and dance the dance of radiance.

This dance is not for the heavy-footed. You will have to lift both feet simultaneously and commit to becoming airborne. You will have to sway and fall back without always knowing for certain that there is someone to catch you, or something to break your fall. You will have to trust.

Nevertheless, you will be captivated by the dare to take flight and free-fall. Gravity's hold has got nothing on you, not when you are all set to give rise to nascent, nocturnal visions. Heaven becomes earth and up morphs into down, when you are dancing the dance of radiance. You hear the pulsating rhythms of your own life. You begin to feel the carefully orchestrated steps of a tap, a soft shoe, a tango, a waltz. You remember to hand over the lead to your partner. It's so easy to dip and bend when God is leading the way across the terrain of your lives. You glide into glory.

PEAK SPEAK

I allow the spirit of adventure and trust to guide my every step. I partner up with God in every area of my life!

Summer Solstice of the Soul

NOW IS THE SEASON of our joyous content! It is the time when we remember that we know that we know that we know. We remember that everything is cyclical and that not only is change possible, it's guaranteed. We remember that what may appear to be a dark night of the soul—those times when we walk into the caves of our fears and peel away layers of self-condemnation and untruths—are actually good God-glory moments. We remember that in the end, the only prayer to utter is a thank you: "Thank you, God, for every hurdle and every leap. I could not have made one without the other."

As we enter the summer solstice of the soul, time collapses. It's the longest day of our life's journey, and also the shortest. For the truth is, there is no time in God and space; there is only the Right Now.

So where are you *right now*? What buried treasure within your soul wants to be excavated in this new season of your life? What desire is hoping to be ignited by your fiery compassionate passion? What secret dream longs to blare through the universe, mix with the music of the spheres and harmonize with all that is good and true and pure of heart?

Take this moment, this endless time filled with endless love, to ponder the inevitable: You have all that you need to bring this desire out from the consecrated shadows and into the sacred light of day. You are absolutely ready and prepared to birth this vision that has been beckoning you for a lifetime, for God is loving you through every contraction. So why not just do it now?

PEAK
SPEAK

I am resolute in the absolute truth that with God working through and as me, I can do everything and anything! Time stands still for my soul.

Everything

Dear Beloved,

I am your true north, south, east and west. I walk
with you and I talk with you—through the night and into
morning's grace. You may want to toss and turn your
fears into bridges to nowhere, but I am here. See. Me.
Now.

I am everything and nothing and no thing. I seek you
in eight billion beings, and in the intricacies of every solar
system. I spin myself into ecstasy when another possibility,
a new idea, is birthed. You declare: I am here and I will
make a life and do great things—build and destroy, make
love and war, be born and return to the beginning.
Ashes into dust into Spirit once again.

And through it all, I am loving you. I outstretch my
majesty toward you and invite and invoke and evoke:
Rise in love! Pick up your bed and walk and skip and run!
Leap into the unknown! Heal yourselves of the belief that
you are unworthy. Disavow yourselves of the notion
that I have abandoned you or forsaken you for another.

There are two ways of seeing: with the body and with the soul. The body's sight can sometimes forget, but the soul remembers forever.

ALEXANDRE DUMAS

For in my eyes, there is only you. I have poured all of my love into you. Your cup runneth over, blessing every-one. Love burnishes and purifies, rectifies and sanctifies. It will not be contained. It expands and overtakes your fears. It fertilizes fields of indecision and doubt. If you let it, if you let me.

Love stands at the door and knocks. It will be there when you are ready, awaiting your acceptance and your salvation. Love is who and what I am. Therefore, it is who and what you are. I want to know you this day—wholly, completely, in all ways. I want you to remember me. I want you to love me as I love you.

Love,
God In You and As You

PEAK SPEAK

I rise in love when I trust in the Ineffable Presence all around me. I am worthy to be loved. I am love itself!

Love Without Limits

HEED THE CALL! A mighty love yearns to frolic with you, imbed itself in you, then synchronize its harmonies with your DNA. Love Unlimited is beckoning you in waves. Let it wash over you, let it penetrate you until you can no longer recall a moment when you were not always ebbing and flowing. Dams be damned! You are holy, wholly streaming.

Be in your knowing. Remember who you are and why you are here.

Dive deep then soar higher than wings can carry you. Yours will not melt like Icarus'. Instead, you will become one with the sun.

Do not go gentle into that good night. Instead, create a spark, a star, a meteor shower that will illuminate the hearts and souls of everyone you encounter.

Bind any lingering doubts into sheaves of laughter and jettison them now. They do not serve you. Extend your arms in a pose of receptivity even when you fear you might walk away empty-handed. Bounty awaits you.

The eye with which I see God is the same with which God sees me. My eye and God's eye is one eye, and one sight, and one knowledge, and one love.

MEISTER ECKHART

Embrace the tremendous opportunities life is offering you right now, and know that you can not make a bad choice because the universe is course corrective. It aligns to your highest and most glorious interests—and is very interested in you, *all* of you.

Hesitate no more. Dare. Surrender. Allow. Release.

Let love! Revel in your wonder. Be vigilant—about you. Let love do the thinking and the planning, the dipping and the diving, the rising and the rectifying. It has a way of revealing the essence of everything, and right now and for eternity, love is loving you.

PEAK
SPEAK

I am led by love. Everything I am is love. Everything I do is love. Love rules!

Aftermath

Bow DOWN, NOW, on your knees and in your hearts. Feel the rock-hard earth yield to the weight of the burdens you have chosen to taken on and carry in your soul. Let the soil fall through your fingertips and remember: It has always been up to you. And now, you can let it all go.

Through it all, deep down you have always known, and now you get to reveal your awareness, your gifts, your insights and your radiance. You are fiercely faithful and you embody the ebullient grace—and the grit—of the journey.

And what a journey it's been! You are a loving testament to the grace that permeates everything alive and activated. You have gasped and exclaimed, cried and shouted, and lamented over what you could have, should have, done. You have dived deep into canyons and reservoirs of resistance, and risen like the phoenix, majestic and shimmering. You have leaped over thresholds you perceived to be barriers but were in fact catalysts for your dynamic emergence. You have danced with the Divine and brought forth a lifetime of experiences and divinations. Now, you are soaring!

Up, up and away upon rungs that ring in anticipation of your grace, your beauty and your vivacious spirit! Up, up and away into the highest tiers of your consciousness where you stand face to face with the Divine and celebrate the essence of your being!

You can let it all go—the doubt, the fear, the self-flagellation. There is no need to hide your glory any longer. Instead, accept the truth of you, and relish the promises intrinsic to you. Life is for you and you are all-powerful.

PEAK
SPEAK

I rejoice in the surrendering of my soul as I open up to the truth of who I really am! I love me!

Look Homeward, Angel

ALLOW A SENSE OF PLACE to anchor you. This place does not have a particular longitude or latitude. It does not know north from south, or east from west. It is both near and far, it is beyond the horizons and beyond the beyond.

Your true home encompasses diverse landscapes. From Forest, Plateau, Tundra, Valley, Riverbank, Garden, Ocean, Mountaintop to Vastness, you will find solace in all of them. Every landscape beckons and has riches for you to excavate. Insight. Wonder. Ecstasy.

It is not the destination that matters so much as the joy you express as you make your way home. And to home you will inevitably return, whether you are a believer or a non-believer, whether you pray, meditate or medicate. Home to where we merge with the essence of who we truly are. Home to where we resonate with the music of the spheres and feel every atom, every strand of DNA, every feather, every leaf. We tremble in anticipation of the glory we are and have always been.

We bow down and the entire universe kneels at our feet.

This pilgrimage is for those who are willing to massage their own hearts into a deep abiding love. We go gentle into our own human existence, forgiving ourselves for forgetting our divinity and our dignity. We forgive everyone we meet, judge, criticize and chastise. We learn to love.

It is only then that we remember the soft sounds of our mother's wombs. Only then can we recreate the moment in which we came to inhabit the body, sequestering our souls within human form. Limbs. Organs. Blood. Marrow. Muscle. We luxuriate in the memory of love becoming life, and life becoming love. Life is unfolding and we are unfolding along with it. Home, at last.

PEAK
SPEAK

I relish and cherish every encounter, every experience, every landscape of my soul.
Life is always carrying me home!

Closing Blessing

Benediction

May you feel the presence of God this and every day.

May you know that everything down to every nanosecond in your life is divinely orchestrated. You are not alone and never have been. Ever.

May your heart continue to expand so that you allow God's grace to overflow.

May your sorrows be given room to breathe and alchemize.

May your joys feel boundless and free.

May your emotions signal and signify, leading you down paths well traveled and less so so that you can heal.

May your cogent beliefs turn you upside down and inside out as you question and then release them. Let go of any and all attachments to thought.

May you fertilize your dreams with love instead of fear.

May you know that you are possibility and that you are pregnant with life, insight and revelation. You are always creating.

May you revolutionize your doubts so that they line up in synchronized arrangements, creating a web of support.

The earth was all before me. With a heart
Joyous, nor scared at its own liberty,
I look about; and should the chosen guide
Be nothing better than a wandering cloud,
I cannot miss my way.

WILLIAM WORDSWORTH

May you know infinite prayer and praise. You have come to sing new worlds into existence.

May you remember your purpose and passions in the face of all that happens to you and through you. You are creating our experiences. You are building a life.

May seamless friendships weave you into a place of wholeness.

May you lean into the field of endless love and pour even more love into it, build a fortress of faith that sustains the tiniest of mustard seeds.

May you know that when you shout and scream your rage—both audibly and silently—you are heard. You are loved.

May you find solace in your connection to all expressions of the Divine. You are part of a holy whole. Again, you are not alone.

May you thrive and bless, for you are pure blessing.

PEAK
SPEAK

I live a life filled with love and grace! I am open to receiving and to giving, to being a blessing and to being blessed. And so it is. Amen.

Acknowledgments

THANK YOU, SPIRIT, for giving me the words to write, and for the synapses and the synchronicities to connect the dots. I am grateful to be an instrument. I am grateful for our connection.

To my sister Charlayne Jones and to my brothers Sean and Ivan Brailsford, proof that smarts, insight and a wicked sense of humor are ninety-nine percent genetic: Thank you for laughter and collective memory and endless text message threads.

To my soul sisters and brothers and magnificent friends Precious Stone, Nargess Mozafari, Pamela Whitman, Crystal Chan, Katherine Dunham, Alexandra Enders, Monica Clark, Brantley Bardin, Mimi DiTrani, Diana Deene, Karen Springen, Genea Tafesse, Michael Dyer, Marilyn White, Mary Weems and Mitch Earle, and to my beloved Sacred Circle, most notably Brian Walton and gracious hosts Chemin and Stanley Bernard: Thank you for your love and support.

Since I began writing *Sacred Landscapes*, a few souls dear to me have walked through the veil to the other side. To Christopher Martin Quander, CJ Felton and Deborah Baron: May you rest and dance in peace and power.

Thank you to Mary Frances Dunham, one of the kindest beings I know. As a sixth grader, I realized that she, an atheist, would not end up in a fiery pit. Because of her, I was guided to find God, in the words of Ntozake Shange, in myself.

Thank you to Rev. Michael Bernard Beckwith for uniting the world in Agape love. And to Rev. Mary Miller for always being so appreciative of my submissions to *Inner Visions*.

I am especially grateful to Lisa Poliak, Addette Williams and Robyn Henry Crittenden, who over the years inquired, "Karen, where is your book?" And to Rev. Greta Sesheta, a brilliant writer who once told me "the world is waiting" for this particular one.

To my agent, friend and Yale classmate, Todd Shuster, who guided me tremendously in structuring *Sacred Landscapes*, and to Aevitas Creative Management colleagues Jennifer Gates and Erica Bauman for their invaluable input.

To publisher Nancy Cleary, who infused that structure with brilliant design, leading the still, small voice to declare "It's perfect" when I first held this book in my hands.

To Beth Grossman, publicist and synchronicity soul sister who really does "make things happen," all with a sense of infectious awe and wonder.

To an immensely dear heart, phenomenal editor and doubting Thomas, Stephen O'Shea: Thank you for reading (and re-reading) *Sacred Landscapes* during its gestation.

Deepest appreciation and love "all the way to the far, far, far, far...Milky Way" for my amazing daughter, Amandla Stenberg, whom I sang spontaneously into existence with a rendition of "Bringing in the Sheaves." Thank you to your soul for entrusting me to be your mama. I have been rejoicing ever since.

About the Author

Writer, editor, spiritual guide and intuitive creator
Karen Brailsford has worked on staff at *Newsweek*, *Elle*,
People, *In Touch* and E! Entertainment covering arts and
culture, Hollywood, fashion, beauty and human interest.
Her writing has also appeared in *The New York Times Book
Review*, *Black Enterprise*, *Interview* and other publications.
A native New Yorker, Karen is a graduate of The Brearley
School and Yale. Her paintings have been exhibited at
Bergamot Station in Santa Monica, California, and else-
where. Karen lives in Los Angeles, the City of Angels,
where she is a licensed spiritual practitioner with the
Agape International Spiritual Center. Paris, the City of
Light, is her go-to landscape.

Visit her website at www.karenbrailsford.com.

Permissions

CPSIA information can be obtained
at www.ICGtesting.com
Printed in the USA
BVHW020157180322
631666BV00006B/284

9 781948 018845